CITIES AND CANOPIES

With best wishes

PRAISE FOR THE BOOK

'*Cities and Canopies* is packed with fun facts, engaging stories, and superb tales and factoids about Indian city trees'—Pradip Krishen, author, environmentalist and film-maker

'Just try this: Walk by or be driven through any city, refusing flatly to look at any building or read any hoarding, with your gaze fixed only on the trees you pass. The impact is amazing. They embrace you, engulf you and transport you into the world of their fragile fascination and that of our life in nature. Harini Nagendra and Seema Mundoli do precisely that through this gripping journey into the world of trees, so close to us and yet so spurned by our cement minds and steel eyes. One closes this book with just one thought: thank you, trees, for just being what you are, where you are'—Gopalkrishna Gandhi, former IAS officer and former governor of West Bengal

'*Cities and Canopies* is a splendid book about trees and their many associates, ranging from birds and bats, wasps and ants to skinks and snakes, with fascinating titbits about science, such as how trees communicate with each other with the help of the fungal network connecting their roots; about history, such as how Kabir's great banyan tree on Kabirwad Island in Bharuch might in fact be much older and be the one that Alexander described; about how humans relate to trees, including their roles in games and art; their medicinal uses and how to concoct a jamun squash. A very enjoyable read that I highly recommend to all lovers of nature, culture and food'—Madhav Gadgil, ecologist, writer and columnist

'This book challenges the urban–rural divide in our minds. It helps city dwellers understand the dangers of nature-deficit disorder and rediscover the biophilia—a love for nature—that exists in us all. Harini Nagendra and Seema Mundoli do this with joy, professionalism and deep knowledge. They introduce us to the secret language of nature, such as the silent communication between the glorious amaltas tree and its carpenter bee pollinators. They frame interesting questions such as can urban trees communicate with each other as well as those in forests? They also help us re-examine our animosity towards immigrant species, reminding us that the "sriphala" (the sacred coconut) and our very own tamarind are in fact exotics. A feast of a book, *Cities and Canopies* is timely and important for young people to read, and act upon'—Rohini Nilekani, philanthropist, journalist, author and social activist

'The book is a luscious romp through the fruit, fun, poetry, folk tales, history and healing properties of the trees we live with'—*Live Mint*

'Those who see timber in trees (and electricity in rivers) should read a book, just out, that can only be described as beautiful. Harini Nagendra and Seema Mundoli have given us a riveting work—*Cities and Canopies: Trees in Indian Cities*'—Scroll.in

'*Cities and Canopies* is a fresh, breezy cocktail—one that lifts your spirits yet strikes a note of melancholy, rekindling lost loves and associations, kindling new knowledge and wonder, as it maps the ecological and cultural histories of trees in cities and in our lives, past and present'—*Hindustan Times*

'The book will take you on a tour of the familiar as well as the unknown'—*Week*

'The writing is simple and straightforward throughout—and frankly this is a book that ought to be made mandatory reading for all school children and adults'—*Open*

'With an easy style of writing and by breaking down scientific facts into relatable bits of information, the authors make the book accessible to a wide audience'—Mongabay

'*Cities and Canopies*, written by Harini Nagendra and Seema Mundoli, reveals myriad facts about the trees we've grown up watching and also gives us a painful reminder of their importance, given the tree-starved state of our urban landscape'—*Financial Express*

'Through a blend of science, history, memory and whimsy, *Cities and Canopies* draws lucid sketches of the most common trees found in Indian cities and the life-systems they support'—*Indian Express*

'With thousands of trees being felled in New Delhi, this is a key reminder of what the urban canopy does for the environment and for us'—*Nature*

'A new book [that] combines scientific rigour with anecdotes and nostalgia to highlight the significance of trees in urban life'—*Forbes*

'It documents the intersection of history, culture and ecology in urban India through trees'—*New Indian Express*

CITIES AND
CANOPIES
Trees in Indian Cities

Harini Nagendra
and Seema Mundoli

PENGUIN
VIKING

An imprint of Penguin Random House

VIKING

USA | Canada | UK | Ireland | Australia
New Zealand | India | South Africa | China

Viking is part of the Penguin Random House group of companies
whose addresses can be found at global.penguinrandomhouse.com

Published by Penguin Random House India Pvt. Ltd
7th Floor, Infinity Tower C, DLF Cyber City,
Gurgaon 122 002, Haryana, India

First published in Viking by Penguin Random House India 2019

ISBN 9780670091218

Typeset in Paciencia by Manipal Digital Systems, Manipal
Printed at Thomson Press India Ltd, New Delhi

www.penguin.co.in

For three generations of my family who love trees:
my grandmother, Thungabai; my mother, Manjula; and my
daughter, Dhwani
Harini

To the frangipani tree of my childhood on whose branches my
brother and I spent summer afternoons lazing, reading and
planning our next adventure
Seema

CONTENTS

ONE

A
KHICHRI
OF TREES

Most of our grandparents were born in the villages of India—
most of our grandchildren will be born in its cities. The
entire world is experiencing a massive shift towards cities, and
India is very much a part of this trend. One in every three Indians
already lives in cities. In twenty to twenty-five years, one out of
every two Indians will live in cities, with the total population in
cities more than doubling in this short span.

This fast growth of cities puts incredible pressure on the
country's ecology, as forests disappear, rivers and wetlands shrink
into thin polluted slivers, and vistas of green and blue turn into
horizons of concrete. But India's cities are not divorced from nature.
In fact, many of them are now greener than their surrounding
areas. Over centuries, they have been assiduously planted with
trees, greened and nurtured by successive kings and commoners.

India's cities derive so much of their character, identity
and liveability from the trees that grow there. From tree-lined
streets where we shop for vegetables and clothes to wooded parks

and playgrounds where children play and adults gather to walk while they talk and sacred trees at intersections where nature is worshipped in the heart of the madding crowd—our cities would be unrecognizable, unliveable, without their trees.

Human choices and historical events have shaped the set of trees we see in each city. Most texts about ancient India describe towns encircled by rows of thorny trees, planted close together to protect the city from invasion. Within the city, public parks and waterbodies were landscaped with trees and flowering plants, while wealthy and royal households maintained residential gardens for private enjoyment. Orchards of fruiting trees provided fruit and income, while temples had groves of fruiting and flowering trees and plants. At street corners large trees were strategically planted, with platforms under them where people could sit together. Groves of large sacred trees like banyan and peepul provided serene sanctuaries outside the city walls, inhabited by saints and philosophers.

Other rulers entered with their influences. The Mughals brought in the idea of the Persian and Islamic gardens, which other rulers like Hyder Ali and Tipu Sultan took to Mysuru, and the kings of the Bahmani Sultanate to the Deccan Plateau. The Marathas had their own style of gardens, as did the Rajputs. Portuguese, French and British colonialists added their own influences. In modern times, industrialists and landscapers have even brought in influences of faux Californian landscapes all the way from Silicon Valley. Our cities are now a fascinating mishmash, a khichri of trees, built on a base of local dal and rice but constantly infused with new ingredients and spices imported from different parts of the world.

We cannot imagine a life without trees. But trees mean different things to different people. A beautiful sequence in

Asvaghosha's *Buddhacarita* (a first–second century CE poem on Gautama Buddha's life) describes women pointing out the trees in the garden of Padmakhanda, just outside the Sakya capital of Kapilavastu, to the Buddha.

> See, my lord, this mango loaded with honey-scented flowers, in which the koel calls, looking as if imprisoned in a golden cage.
> Look at this Asoka tree, the increaser of lovers' sorrows, in which the bees murmur as if scorched by fire.
> Behold this Tilaka tree, embraced by a woman with yellow body-paint. See the Kurubaka in full bloom, shining like lac just squeezed out, which bends over as if dazzled by the brilliance of the women's nails.
> And look at this young Asoka tree, all covered with young shoots, which stands as if abashed by the glitter of our hands.

The romantic image of trees that this poem conjured was very different from the directions of Buddha's thoughts. He retreated from this conversation, eventually renouncing the city altogether and making his way to the forest in search of a higher truth.

Trees mean different things to different people — for some they are prosaic sources of fruit and wood, while for others they offer beautiful flowers that fascinate and dazzle, philosophic places of contemplation or something entirely different. All shades for all people, often bringing multiple meanings to the same person as well.

As a resident of Bengaluru memorably put it in one of the city's many tree events, 'Who would be foolish enough to dislike a tree?' referring to us, the audience of tree lovers gathered at the meeting.

Indeed.

We write this book as two city dwellers who love trees. We hope that you find something of your interest tucked in the pages of this book. Trees in Indian cities are an endangered lot. The older and more beautiful the trees in a city, the more likely it seems that they are in the firing line — cut down to make way for a wider road, metro line, apartment building or a mall. Citizen protests and community pressure seem to be the only way to save trees. Information is a key to this battle, but so is emotion.

This is not a field guide to trees in a specific city. There are a number of books on Indian cities, such as Pradip Krishen's much-admired *Trees of Delhi*, that do this so well. Nor is it a botany book aimed at the tree expert. There are excellent books of this kind too. This is a fun book on trees in India's cities — a book that you can read and relate to, no matter which part of the country you come from or live in. We hope that dipping into this book will satisfy your thirst. At the same time, we wish that it stimulates your interest in knowing more about your city and its trees, and makes you take a stroll or two around your neighbourhood over the weekend to go tree spotting with friends and family.

At the same time, as is inevitable in any book, and even more so in a book of this nature, we cannot hope to cover it all. We do not try to — this is a sampler, not an exhaustive tome. If we were to discuss all the trees found in all the cities of India, this would be a many volume encyclopedia. Even all the common trees would be difficult to cover, as different trees would be common in different parts of the country. Instead, the book talks of some of the most frequent and characteristic species, to provide a flavour common to multiple cities.

Trees in cities are much more than just the name tags or species identities they carry. Associated with trees are ideas of games and food, assemblages of insects and monkeys, identities of sacred and secular, heated debates about native and foreign origin, and even mental disorders such as the intriguingly named nature-deficit disorder. We cover a range of these aspects in this book, which alternates between chapters focused on specific species and on themes of this kind. As two ecologists who study the history of nature in cities, this book contains many of our favourite stories — tales of fascinating ecologies, evolutionary battles with pollinators, and historical encounters with kings and commoners. At the same time, it is very much a book written by two women, as you will see, with our favourite games, recipes, recommendations for home-made hair oil, poems and stories thrown in too.

This book is for those who love their trees and are passionate defenders of their right to exist, and it is for those who like trees but are not really convinced that the city is the right place for them. After all, trees are many things to many people. Whatever your position on trees though, we hope to leave you with food for thought and a deeper appreciation of our emotional and evolutionary connect to these sublime creations that have been around for far longer than us on this earth.

TWO

JAMUN: THE TREE
AT THE CENTRE
OF THE WORLD

Laden with purple fruits that stain the sidewalks and our mouths, the jamun tree is a favourite in Indian cities. It is found across most parts of the country and is native to the Indian subcontinent.

The tree is central to the cosmology of Hinduism, Jainism and Buddhism — three major religions that took root from this region. Though they differ in details, all three describe the ancient world as being composed of a number of *dwipa*s (island continents). One of the most important of these islands is the Jambudwipa, the island of the jamun trees. In the *Vishnu Purana*, Jambudwipa, which was the central of seven islands, is described with *jambu* (jamun) trees that bore fruits as large as elephants. When the ripe massive fruits fell from the trees on to the mountain tops, the juice flowed from them in torrents, forming the Jambunadi. This river of jamun juice flowed through the island and was enjoyed by all its inhabitants.

The jamun tree is not just characteristic of ancient and mythological India. It appears in the chronicles of many travellers, both Indian and foreign. Ancient Sanskrit medical texts by Charaka, Susruta and Vagbhata describe the use of the jamun as a cure for vomiting in babies, spider bites and an assortment of other diseases and disorders. In the Ramayana, Rama and Sita are believed to have feasted on jamuns during their long years of exile.

Jamuns played a prominent role in the life of the second Avvaiyar, a revered Tamil poetess-saint. An often-told story of Muruga (Kartikeya) begins with Avvaiyar sitting under a jamun tree, when she sees a young shepherd. Feeling hungry, she asks him for some fruit. He responds by asking '*Sutta pazham? Sudatha pazham?*' (Do you want the fruit to be hot [roasted] or cool [uncooked]?). Thinking that he was a simple, uneducated boy asking her a silly question, Avvaiyar responded that, of course, she wanted the cool, uncooked fruit. When he shook the branches of the tree, the fruit fell on to the ground below. She picked up the fruit and blew on it to remove the sand. He laughed and asked her, 'What happened? Why are you blowing on the fruit to cool it? Is it hot?' Struck by the ease with which he had tricked her, she asked who he was. The shepherd boy revealed himself to be Lord Muruga.

Popular across Tamil Nadu, the story made its way into a classic Tamil movie of 1953 with the same name, *Avvaiyar*. This encounter with a child, who was not what he seemed to be, led Avvaiyar to begin writing for children. She composed a number of books with insightful sayings for children. These compositions continue to be popular across Tamil Nadu till date, just as the movie *Avvaiyar* whose scene under the jamun tree continues to be widely watched with close to 500 million views on YouTube.

Avvaiyar's life-changing encounter under the jamun tree is believed to have taken place sometime in the tenth century CE, during the reign of the Cholas. Well before this, Chinese monk Fa-Hsien, who visited India between 399 AD and 414 AD, mentioned the jamun tree, as did Hiuen Tsang who was in the subcontinent sometime between 629 AD and 245 AD. In 1333, Ibn Battuta described the tree, with fruits 'like the olive', black and with a single stone, in Muhammad bin Tughlaq's Delhi.

Babur, who ruled the areas around Delhi two centuries after Tughlaq, did not think much of the jamun. He was a man of decided opinions, declaring the mango to be the best fruit of Hindustan and speaking highly of the banana. In his memoirs, he acknowledged that the jamun tree was 'fine looking', but the fruit, which resembled that of a black grape, 'has a more acidic taste and is not very good'.

The bitter taste that Babur disliked so much comes from the high tannin content of the fruit. Tannins, or polyphenol, are found in many health foods ranging from the jamun to red grapes, wine, dark chocolate and black tea. They leave a bitter sensation in the mouth and a puckered-up feeling on the tongue by binding with our saliva and drying out the mouth. It is the tannins that give the jamun its peculiar medicinal properties. Some scientists refer to tannins as a double-edged sword—too much can reduce our ability to absorb iron and vitamins from food and even stimulate some forms of cancer. But in small amounts, tannins are good for us. In fact, they prevent some cancers, protects us from microbial and fungal infections and offer a host of other health benefits. Hence the New Age endorsement of wine, chocolate and jamun as health foods.

Jamun, if you are in the know, seems to be capable of addressing almost every health disorder known to humankind. And it's not just the tannins at work. The fruit's purple colour comes from its characteristic pigment, anthocyanins. Antioxidants, anthocyanins are also found in blueberries, cranberries and purple cabbage—all exotic superfoods now being touted as miracle cures against varied diseases such as cancer and dementia. But there's no need to go looking for imported blueberries when you have the humble jamun closer to home. Sirka (jamun vinegar), made by leaving jamun pulp to ferment with sugar for several weeks followed by straining, is an excellent salad dressing and offers a healthy home-made substitute to balsamic vinegar.

The fruit, bark, seeds, and even the leaves, are anti-diabetic. In fact, all parts of the tree have medicinal properties. The jamun is used widely in Ayurveda and by traditional healers across the country. The diluted juice can be used as a gargling solution to ward off infections, while the same juice, if applied on the skin and scalp, can be used locally to treat ringworm infections. The pulp can also be used to treat mouth ulcers and gum bleeds. The bark and the inner hard seeds, once dried and powdered, can fight internal disorders like dysentery. The seeds can also be ground into a paste and used in face packs to treat acne and pimples. The astringent juice of the fruit makes for an excellent ingredient in face packs, but only as long as you remember to wash it off well, else you will be left with a purple-tinged face for a few days.

The jamun is also a tree with high-tech possibilities. Recent research by scientists at the Indian Institute of Technology (IIT), Roorkee, suggests that the anthocyanins extracted from jamuns can be used to manufacture dye-sensitized solar cells at a lower cost. Another group of scientists at IIT Hyderabad used activated carbon, derived from powdered jamun seeds, to remove fluoride from contaminated water. If this technology can be scaled up and perfected, it can be a low-cost, simple way to supply drinking water to India's fluorosis-affected villages.

Given its many uses, it is no surprise that the jamun is so widespread across India. It is an ideal tree to plant in commons and public land, as it grows easily, thrives even in dry soil and requires little watering after the initial months. It is incredibly long-living with one tree capable of providing fruits to multiple generations. The wood is somewhat hard and difficult to carve, but is sought-after in villages to make agricultural implements, carts and rudimentary furniture. It is also used in building wells as the wood is water-resistant. In the wild, the tree can grow up to 90 feet in height. Though shorter in cities, it can still grow to massive heights. The shelter of the jamun tree is particularly coveted in the summer. The evergreen tree, covered in leaves all through the year, usually has a large canopy that acts like a massive umbrella.

It is common to find jamuns on the road and in roadside fields and maidans under which a cluster of street vendors, picnickers and children congregate in the summer months. Many sacred locations across India are also shaded by a heritage jamun tree, such as the southern temple city of Srirangam, contributing to the characteristic atmosphere of calm and peace. The gorgeous, rich purple colour of the fruit is equated to the skin colour of Rama and Krishna, which is why it is common to find a jamun tree in temples dedicated to them.

Bees feast on the nectar produced by the greenish-white, club-shaped, feathery blossoms of the tree. Jamun honey, which these bees produce, has a bitter taste and a characteristic aroma that reminds you of the berries. This honey is much sought-after by diabetics and those with liver disorders. The fruits, when they emerge, are green and oval-shaped. Once they ripen, they turn a beautiful glossy pinkish-purple. The fruit is high in vitamin C, iron and a number of other minerals. Unlike most other fruits, it is also low in sugar and hence is recommended for older people and diabetics. The fruit holds a special place in the memory of all those who have grown up in its surroundings. Unlike Babur, the ripe fruit is very popular with most Indians. They are in fact harvested by street vendors and sold on the roadside with black salt, staining faces, hands and lips with the characteristic purple.

Birds, fruit bats, monkeys and jackals gorge on the fruit, leaving the pavements along many a concrete road purple. Children vie for the ripened fruits, and it is common to see them nimbly shimmy up the tree, cloth bag in hand, to pluck the ripe fruits. Often you may also spot four people, each holding the corner of a large bedsheet, standing eagerly under the branches, while a fifth, perched on the jamun tree above, shakes its branches so that the ripe fruit falls on to the sheet. The fruits bruise easily, so they need to be collected with care. Also, it is difficult to ripen the fruits once they are off the tree. They are mostly plucked when ripe, which also means they need to be consumed relatively fast. Fortunately, all fruits on the tree do not ripen at the same time and a single tree can reliably provide ripe fruits at regular intervals for several weeks during the summer.

From Bengaluru to New Delhi, street vendors sell jamun fruits in purple heaps and happy customers take them home to feast on. As children, it was a favourite pastime of ours to eat jamuns and then stick out our purple-stained tongues and leer at each other, exposing our purple lips and bared teeth. The fruit, however, is the despair of parents who have to deal with the unwelcome task of removing the indelible stains from clothes. In New Delhi, the jamun trees that line both sides of Rajpath all the way to India Gate are believed to supply 500 tonnes of fruit each year. In a practice begun in the times of the British Raj, the fruit is 'owned' by the city administration, which sells licences to families of itinerant fruit pickers who come into the city during summer from the villages around. They sleep under the trees at night and sit under them during the day, guarding the fruit from bats, parakeets, monkeys and other competitors.

Interestingly, different sizes of jamun fruit can be seen on sale. There are a number of local varieties of trees across the country, growing wild in jungles and planted in farms and on common land. The smaller fruits must be eaten with salt, which helps counter the astringent aftertaste and prevents your throat from seizing up. Larger-sized glossy fruits come from a different variety of trees. These are often especially grown in farms and brought to wholesale markets. From there they are taken to street corners for sale to picky urban folk obsessed with size and shape. These modified varieties are usually sweeter and, mixed with sugar, can be used to make juices, smoothies and sorbets. The Goans even make a delicious wine with it, but local wisdom has it that the large-sized fruits are not as good for health as the native smaller berries. They lack the astringent taste because they have less tannins, but this also reduces their medicinal properties.

The jamun is truly a miracle tree. It may not be at the centre of the world in modern cosmology, but it certainly holds importance in India's cities and in our taste buds.

Jamun (*Syzygium cumini*)

Description: Tall tree with a dense shady canopy. Light grey, rough bark, especially the lower part of the trunk.

Flowers: Small, greenish-white flowers that grow in clusters and have a faint fragrance.

Fruits: Oblong-shaped with a single seed. Green when unripe and changes hue as it ripens from pink to purplish-black. Edible fleshy pulp with a tart taste.

Leaves: Smooth, leathery and shining with pointed tips. When crushed, the leaves give out an aroma.

Seasonality: Evergreen, but sheds some leaves in dry climate — leaves normally fall between January and March. Flowers usually between March and May, and fruits ripen from June to August.

Family: Myrtaceae. Leaves and stems of this family have aromatic oil glands.

Origin and distribution: Native to India. Found across the Indian subcontinent and especially abundant in south India, but not so much in the arid regions.

Jamun Kala-Khatta

This popular summer drink is a refreshing antidote for heat strokes. Very easy to make, it is also a great way to benefit from the medicinal properties of jamun, especially for those who find the fruit difficult to consume because of its astringent aftertaste. Though you can opt for the kala-khatta available on the street, you can easily make it at home too. It can be had as a *gola* with shaved ice, as a post-fasting nutritious iftar sherbet during Ramadan, or frozen into cubes and then whipped into a sorbet, slushy or frosty. It is definitely tastier and far more nutritious than the processed stuff you get in high-end stores. You can also experiment with other recipes to make jamun vinegar, jam and wine too.

Recipe:

- 1 cup jamun (cut and deseeded)
- 1 cup water, or soda if you prefer
- 2 tablespoons sugar (or more, to taste)
- 1 pinch salt
- ¼ – ½ teaspoon black salt
- ½ teaspoon roasted cumin powder
- Freshly squeezed lime or orange juice (optional, to cut the astringency)

Blend and strain using a coarse tea strainer. Yes, it's that simple. Now the base is ready and can be turned into a number of different cooling, slushy drinks and desserts.

To make a refreshing sherbet, add ice and pour into a tall glass. You can garnish it with mint leaves. (If you want to get fancy, dip the rim of the glass in a mix of rock salt and black salt before you fill it and serve.) To make a gola, fill a shot glass with shaved ice. Pack it around an ice cream stick (or just use a spoon if you are feeling lazy), carefully pour the juice around the edges of the glass and let it soak into the ice.

For a sorbet, heat the juice for a few minutes (this is optional as this step helps reduce the astringent taste) and then cool or take the raw juice and freeze for an hour. After this, blend in a mixer or food processor. Freeze again and repeat blending after an hour. Pour into a bowl or a wide-mouthed glass and garnish with fresh mint. For a slush, pour the juice mix (cooked and cooled if you prefer) into an ice-cube tray. Take out the jamun ice cubes and process in a mixer or food processor. If you prefer a frosty, blend the jamun ice cubes with some vanilla ice cream. Use your imagination to create other alternatives.

THREE

ALL
CREATURES
GREAT AND SMALL

If we look out of the window of an aeroplane as it descends into a city, we see the blurry landscape transform into more comprehensible features. Vehicles and people, which appear to be the size of tiny ants scuttling about, progressively begin to take recognizable shape. The same is the case with biodiversity in cities. A perfunctory glance at trees while we travel in a bus or a car, on cycle or on foot, does not reveal the host of activities hidden in the branches, leaves and canopies. But fauna of different kinds go on with their lives, dodging the perils of city life just as we humans dodge traffic. What biodiversity do the trees in our city harbour and where can we find them?

For many nature enthusiasts, the first introduction to nature is through birdwatching, often beginning in the cities in which they live. British naturalists E.H. Aitken (or Eha), David Douglas Cunningham and Douglas Dewar have written about birds in Kolkata, Mumbai and Chennai. The field guides to birds of India written by Salim Ali, the famous Indian naturalist and ornithologist, are indispensable companions for many birdwatchers. Another famous naturalist, photographer and a prolific writer, M. Krishnan, wrote evocative descriptions of his encounters with biodiversity. Interspersed with his characteristic wit, these remain as absorbing as when they were first published. Krishnan held that 'it is a mistake to think that cities hold few birds', and describes his encounters with different birds in Madras, as the city he lived in for much of his life was then known. Krishnan wrote with equal flair about uncommon birds such as the visiting golden-back woodpeckers pecking at the coconut trunks around his house and the common crow that preferred more open parts of the city with less tree growth.

Krishnan's writings provide interesting insights into bird behaviour such as feeding, mating and nesting habits. The coppersmith, he says, 'like all barbets, is strictly arboreal', and is 'fond of the shady sanctuary of fig trees'. It is 'justly called the voice of summer' because it calls in the 'blistering heat of Madras April afternoon'. In just a few words, he tells us so much about the bird. While Krishnan bemoaned the lack of trees in cities, he also hoped that municipalities would plant trees with good foliage in parks and along avenues, so that the trees could attract 'charming and inoffensive' birds such as orioles and flycatchers.

Madras has now become Chennai and many of the tree-lined neighbourhoods that Krishnan wrote about have been transformed by the city's growth. But birdwatching continues to be a popular activity in Chennai and other cities even today. Bird counts held at regular intervals provide an opportunity for enthusiasts to document birds that can still be found in cities. The India Bird Races, started in 2005 in Mumbai, have become immensely popular and are now held across thirteen cities. A typical bird race begins at dawn and ends at dusk. Teams head out in different directions, aiming to record the maximum number of bird species in and around the city. While making a checklist, they also get to network, observe bird behaviour and exchange information about birds.

But we don't really need a race to appreciate our winged friends. We can always indulge in birdwatching by taking a stroll down the closest avenue, around a lake, in a park or even in our own backyards. We can immerse ourselves in trying to spot the now elusive coppersmiths and shikras, or observing the shenanigans of common birds such as crows, black kites and mynas.

Eha makes the crow appear fascinating. Rather ungraciously, he says of the crow that it is a 'fungus of city life, a corollary to man and sin', without a 'shred of grace'. According to Eha, the crow 'affects to be respectable and entirely ignores public opinion, dresses like a gentleman, carries itself jauntily, and examines everything with one eye'. Along with pigeons, crows are the most common of birds in cities. Observing them can be an immense source of entertainment. Crows can be found hopping sideways on the branches of a rain tree or trying to get a firm grip on the swaying fronds of a coconut tree. We may not pay much attention to this very common bird, but urban crows display a range of interesting behaviours while perched on branches such as rousing, feaking and preening. Rousing is when a bird shakes and fluffs its feathers out. This is often done during or after the rains so that the feathers trap air and keep the bird warm, though it also leaves the bird looking rather ridiculous. Feaking is when a crow rubs its beak against the branch — somewhat akin to us brushing our teeth. Preening involves cleaning and adjusting of feathers.

Trees also provide nesting sites for crows, and they often build nests in the unlikeliest of places — we have seen a crow's nest on a jamun tree at a crowded railway platform. Crows are attracted by garbage and can become very aggressive, chasing and mobbing other birds, even much larger birds of prey.

Alongside the raucous call of the crows, the common mynas add their chatter at shared roosting sites in tree foliage as dusk falls. The racket made by these birds settling down for the night can even be heard over the honking of cars. Of mynas, Ranjit Lal says, 'City life suits Indian mynas just fine and they will eat almost anything they can find. But they are also very important pollinators (yes, VIPs) of plants like fig, mulberry and sandal, and are responsible for scattering seeds far and wide.' The fig trees we see growing out of walls, sidewalks and buildings owe their existence to these mynas and other birds.

Another bird that is commonly seen in cities is the black kite. Like the crow, it is a scavenger of the city's garbage dumps. Black kites prefer to perch on the tallest trees they can find, such as silver oak or eucalyptus, keeping a sharp lookout. Any sign of prey and the kite can be seen launching itself—a plunging dive with its wings wide open, followed by an ascent with the measured beating of its wings. The black kite was once known as the pariah kite. The term 'pariah' was used denigratingly, to denote a person from the lower caste treated as a social outcaste. Our nasty social prejudices seem to have extended to the naming of biological species too. While the black kite was made the pariah, the Brahminy kite with its white streaked forehead got its name from the word 'brahmin', alluding to a higher caste status. In Indian mythology, the Brahminy kite is associated with Garuda, the *vahana* (vehicle) of Vishnu. Many traditional communities, even in the heart of a city like Bengaluru, feed the kites with mutton or fish on Saturdays, an act they believe will confer merit on them. Black kite and Brahminy kite nests can be found on trees near waterbodies such as lakes.

There are several other species of birds that bustle about in city trees. We can witness rose-ringed parakeets engaged in courtship displays on African tulips, glimpse red-vented bulbuls flitting in the Indian mast tree, or hear the shrill call of the cuckoo from a neem tree along the road. A mango pecked and dropped by a parakeet is believed to be the tastiest and sought-after by children who swear by the bird's capability to identify the best fruit.

The silk cotton in folklore is termed as a 'parrot's despair'. Folk tales mention parrots eagerly pecking at the tasty looking seed pods and being disappointed to find they contain mostly inedible cotton. But semal flowers provide a feast for birds, who flock in large numbers to the fruiting trees. In larger city parks, spotted and white mottled owls make their home in the hollow of trees, screeching at dusk and glaring indignantly if walkers get too close. With the garbage in cities inviting more rodents, kite and owl populations have also begun to hang about these areas, keeping the rodents in check. Sadly, many of the tall trees in which owls and other birds roost are being destroyed.

But sometimes we are lucky to see rare birds. Recently, a pair of Indian grey hornbills were seen on a peepul tree next to a busy road in Bengaluru, delighting nature lovers in the city. Once commonly found in many Indian cities, the grey hornbills have reduced in numbers as the green spaces in cities have shrunk. Their return to Bengaluru is believed to be because of protected sacred groves and restored lakes. For many years, the Indian Institute of Science campus in Bengaluru was host to a rare breeding pair of Egyptian vultures. There is now a breeding pair in the heart of the city's commercial and shopping district, which is fed chicken by staff from a local restaurant. In Patiala too, the campus of the Punjabi University now boasts of a breeding pair.

Many other birds come to India from different parts of the world. Wintering waterfowl congregate in waterbodies in cities where they nest in scattered trees. In Indian folklore, the pied cuckoo is said to be the harbinger of the monsoon in India. A recent analysis of data from MigrantWatch and eBird, popular citizen science databases used by birdwatchers in India and across the world, shows that the pied cuckoo does seem to arrive in different parts of India before the monsoon. In northern Indian cities sweltering in the summer heat, birdwatchers wait eagerly for the arrival of this bird from Africa. While there is a resident population in south India, in other parts of the country the pied cuckoo is a much-awaited migrant whose metallic calls from treetops are soon followed by rain that progresses along with the bird's flight northwards over the subcontinent.

Wetland birds can also be found in patches in Indian cities. A nature park just outside Kolkata has a large colony of Asian openbills, one of the common but smallest storks found in Asia. These birds have clear preferences when it comes to nesting, favouring trees such as peepul, shisham, copper pod, gulmohar and shirish. Other trees such as neem, cluster fig, tamarind, silk cotton, jamun and Indian beech do not seem to be as preferred. In the coastal town of Kannur in Kerala, heronries can be found on trees situated along roads and next to trees in residential and non-residential areas. Heronry birds such as egrets and herons appear like powder puffs on trees from a distance. They prefer to nest on large canopies of trees such as copper pod, mango, jackfruit and banyan. They also seek out the rain tree whose large branches enable them to build safe nests, and to source dry twigs from the tree for their nests. However, with cities expanding, there are concerns about the continued presence of both the trees and the heronries. The wetlands that the birds accessed are being lost to real estate. The disturbance from construction activity has also resulted in many birds abandoning the nesting sites that they frequented in the past. Urban birds have to be tough and adaptable to find places to perch, nest and roost. Some are able to adapt and find new spaces, but for several others, the loss of trees could mean their very survival being imperilled.

Birds are not the only creatures that make trees their home. Insects, both tiny and large, can also be found on city trees. Some are almost invisible to the naked eye. The rain tree is a common avenue tree in many cities such as Chennai and Bengaluru, with leaves that droop and face sideways (owing to the presence of a pulvinus, or a thickening of the base that enables the leaf to move like a hinge) during the night or on a cloudy day. This has given it the name *thoongumoonji maram* (sleepy-face tree) in Tamil. Sunlight causes the leaves to open up, creating a dense canopy that casts a cooling shade. Some say that the name 'rain tree' comes from the droplets of nectar dropped by sap-sucking insects on the tree in its native habitat.

Flowering trees on avenues are like buffets laid out for a variety of creatures. The African tulip, a common avenue tree, is usually abuzz with activity. The deep red flowers of the African tulip store a small pool of nectar that attracts many insects. The walls of the flowers are sticky, preventing them from getting out. These pools of nectar can therefore prove to be deadly for ants, bees and butterflies who drown in them while trying to access the nectar. Their unfortunate corpses can sometimes be found floating in the nectar. Other insects such as the praying mantis, meanwhile, patiently wait in the African tulip's foliage for prey.

Butterflies of all kinds inhabit our cities. Butterfly walks are held in many cities such as Pune, Bengaluru and New Delhi, and attract crowds of enthusiasts. Many urban naturalist groups have developed small, innovative and colourful field guides to butterflies and birds to attract children and novices to nature in the city. Skinks move swiftly around tree patches, attracting us with a flash of colour as they chase unwary butterflies and other insects. Stick insects, leaf insects and chameleons confuse us with their ability to blend into the background, going unnoticed till they move. Tree frogs with their green or bark-like bodies cling to the bark of trees or green shoots, while snakes of all kinds slither swiftly up and around the bark of trees, sometimes dropping down on the heads of unwary passers-by. If you have had this experience, you will certainly never forget it all your life.

Ants, tiny though they are, constitute nearly 25 per cent of the total animal weight in the tropics. They have also proved to be very versatile, adapting to living in a range of habitats in cities. The weaver ant is a common species of arboreal ant that nests on many types of trees. These ants prepare their nest by carefully weaving together the leaves, coaxing ant larvae to release silk. These nests can be seen on trees in parks if we keep an eye out for leaves that appear to be stuck together. If we are lucky, we can find these built at eye level, allowing us to examine the busy goings-on as ants enter and exit the nest. We may even get to see the nest being built, a fascinating example of cooperation and hard work. But remember to keep a safe distance, the bite from these ants is very painful.

In 1997, researchers discovered a new arboreal ant in Bengaluru. The ant, a spineless two-node variety, was identified as a new species and named *Dilobocondyla bangalorica* in 2007, after the city where it was discovered. This is the first species of this genus to be found in India. This ant prefers to make its nests in the cavities of plumeria and acacia trees. Plumerias are native to the Meso-American and Caribbean region. The gouty-looking plumeria is planted in Hindu and Buddhist temples, as well as in Hindu and

Muslim burial grounds. It is fascinating that a tree from such distant lands has not only become culturally important, but also provides a habitat for an ant species found only in India. Trees of different species also host terrestrial ants that clamber up trees to forage for food and use leaf litter on the base of trees in parks and gardens, and fallen branches as nesting sites. Our first instinct on seeing an ant may be to squish it to avoid being bitten. But if we are patient and tolerant, ant watching like birdwatching can reveal a whole new world to us. Like the new species of ant discovered in Bengaluru, perhaps there are more species waiting to be discovered in cities.

The presence or absence of ants and other critters like tree spiders also tells us about the state of our urban greenery. Ants are extremely adaptable. In disturbed urban areas, the number of species and the number of ants are often higher than in protected sites. However, more common species are found in the disturbed sites while rare species persist in undisturbed areas. Ants act as ecological indicators, telling us about the health of an ecosystem. In urban sacred groves in towns in Kerala, the abundance of the yellow crazy ant, which nests in leaf litter at the base of trees, is indicative of the pressures of urbanization. This ant is an invasive species and its presence indicates a disturbed habitat.

One of the most common mammals we see in cities are squirrels. These striped rodents clamber about branches, chasing each other and snacking on the fruit pods of the African tulip. Bonnet macaques seem to like the succulent buds of the African tulip too, as well as the flowers of the gulmohar. Fruit bats flit about, feasting on fruits of the cluster fig and the Indian mast tree, leaving behind scattered seeds as evidence of their night-time banquets. Some rare species can also be found in the tree canopies of cities. The slender loris is an endangered nocturnal primate that lives in the canopy of trees. At night, this shy primate forages for fruits and insects on treetops and rests in hollows or under leaf cover in the daytime. Though close cousins of the monkey, the slender loris cannot jump from one tree to another and must crawl along the branches. Consequently, it needs a continuous and connected canopy to move from one tree to another.

Young lorises stay in clumps of vegetation created by creepers and vines on trees while the mother loris goes foraging. The slender loris is a species that hardly ever comes to the ground, depending entirely on tree cover to survive. It has been spotted in the heart of busy Bengaluru where there is still continuous tree cover in parks, educational and research institutions. But the cutting of trees and fragmentation of habitats is a major concern for this endangered species. Its survival will depend on how successful we all are in ensuring that the green cover of the city is protected.

All trees in the city, whether on streets, in parks, homes, lakesides or commercial areas, harbour a variety of animal, bird and insect life. From tall coconut palms to spreading rain trees, from exotics such as the sausage tree to the native mango, from the fruiting jackfruit to the flowering African tulip—all trees are home to a variety of biodiversity. Plantation schemes in cities should avoid focusing on single species, whether native or exotic. Instead, a khichri of trees would perhaps support a healthier diversity of fauna.

Above all, trees bring us close to our non-human neighbours. Biophilia, defined by the naturalist E.O. Wilson as 'the innate tendency to focus on life and lifelike processes', is a part of our human identity. It is a love of life that extends beyond caring for humans and embraces all life—animal, bird and insect. Spending more time carefully observing our trees is a good way of reviving the dormant biophilia in each one of us. For school- and college-going students with access to a wooded campus, there is no better way of starting to engage in this process than by looking up at the trees around and observing the animal, bird and insect life that the trees reveal. A love for nature encouraged from a young age can mean a lifetime of caring for our planet.

FOUR

THE SHAGGY-
HEADED
BANYAN TREE

The banyan, the national tree of India, is unforgettable once you see it. With thick aerial roots that grow down from the branches and penetrate the ground, the tree looks like it has many trunks, all collectively holding up its branches with leaves. The banyan has a long and ancient history in India. Alexander the Great, the Greek king who invaded north-west India in the third century BC, is believed to have been struck by the sight of this impressive tree. He sent the news of the banyan tree to his teacher, the famed philosopher Aristotle.

Aristotle's successor and pupil, Theophrastus, also called the Father of Botany, was equally struck by the news of this massive tree. Theophrastus described the banyan in two of the oldest books on plants, *On the Causes of Plants* and the *Enquiry into Plants*, written between the third and second centuries BC. A few centuries later, Roman naturalist Pliny wrote about the tree as being so large that within its branches 'whole troops of horsemen may be concealed'. The tree had captured the romantic imagination of the Europeans.

Spreading like wildfire across Europe, the tale of the charismatic banyan eventually made its way into English poet John Milton's famous poem *Paradise Lost.* In the poem, published in 1667, Adam and Eve made their way:

Into the thickest Wood, there soon they chose
The Figtree, not that kind for Fruit renown'd,
But such as at this day to Indians known
In Malabar or Decan spreds her Armes
Braunching so broad and long, that in the ground
The bended Twigs take root, and Daughters grow
About the Mother Tree, a Pillard shade
High overarch't, and echoing Walks between;
There oft the Indian Herdsman shunning heate
Shelters in coole, and tends his pasturing Herds
At Loopholes cut through thickest shade: Those Leaves
They gatherd, broad as Amazonian Targe,
And with what skill they had, together sowd,
To gird thir waste, vain Covering if to hide
Thir guilt and dreaded shame.

The Europeans were struck by how large the leaves and branches of the banyan tree were and, in comparison, how small the fruit. But these tiny fruits contain a world of mystery within their folds. Sometimes called the world's strangest fruits, the fruits of all ficus trees, commonly called figs, are actually inflorescences (the technical term for these is 'syconia' – an obscure piece of botanical trivia that may come in handy for avid quizzers). Within the fruit are the flowers. If you stop to think, it is strange that the banyan – or indeed the peepul, or any other ficus tree – never seems to bear flowers. In fact, the fruit itself contains a large number of tiny flowers packed tightly inside. These are essential for the pollination of the tree, which is done entirely by wasps.

Vegetarians who eat figs, beware. Many fig fruits are stuffed full of dead wasps. When the fruit is unripe and green, it looks unappetizing to humans but sends out enticing smells that attract a specific kind of wasp—agaonid wasps whose lives are tightly intertwined with that of the fig. Pregnant female wasps, their stomachs bulging with eggs, enter through a small hole at the tip of the fruit. Since the hole is very small, they have to squeeze their bodies through it. It is such a tight fit that their wings and antennae fall off. The unfortunate wasps ultimately die within the fig.

As the fig ripens, the wasp eggs hatch inside the body of the mother, beginning a new cycle of life. The young male and female wasps mate inside the fig. The newly pregnant female wasps then make their way out of a ripe fig and look for an unripe fig to continue the cycle. As they enter another fig, they carry the pollen from the original host on their bodies, pollinating the new host and continuing the process of seed making.

The cycle of the wasp and the fig, both dependent on each other, leads to an unusual outcome. Most trees fruit only at specific times of the year, but not the banyan and other ficus trees. Because the wasps feed only on the figs, and since the wasps are short-lived, the tree needs to continuously produce fruit—so that the wasps always have a source of food available. This prodigious capacity of the ficus trees to produce fruit throughout the year is exploited by many other animals, birds and insects. Giant hornbills, tiny ants, civets, bats, monkeys and slender lorises—all feast on the ficus. In Indian cities, it is common to see a raised platform with a giant banyan tree where people sit comfortably in the shade and enjoy a long chat, a game of cards or chess. The canopy is an equally bustling hive of activity, with chattering birds, monkeys and insects of all shapes and sizes gorging on the fruit. Small wonder that many Indians believe this to be the *kalpavriksha* or *kalpataru*, the wish-fulfilling tree considered sacred in Buddhism, Jainism and Hinduism.

Long before the Vedic texts that describe the kalpavriksha, the Indus Valley civilization may have known the tree. One of their symbols, a stylized three-branched fig tree with lines on each side of the stem, is interpreted by some experts as representing the banyan, with the lines indicating the aerial roots. The proto-Dravidian word for the banyan is *vata maram* (roe tree), as it is still called in Tamil. In Sanskrit, the tree acquires a related name, *vata vriksha*. In Kannada it is the *ala mara*, in Marathi the *vad*, and in Hindi the *bargad*—all related names. Where then did the word 'banyan' come from? The name seems to have been the result of a confusion created by the Portuguese, who noticed banias (traders) often sitting below the tree. They conflated the name of the community with that of the tree. That name passed down from the Portuguese to the British colonials and entered the English language.

It is not only the Indians who venerate the tree. The Indonesian emblem has the banyan tree—its branching roots are believed to represent the many islands that make up the country. The banyan is revered as a symbol of unity, bringing together many different islands with their own cultures, languages and historical roots into a united whole, which is a beautiful concept.

Growing to giant proportions, banyan trees are easy to identify because of their unique aerial roots. These roots arise from the branches of the tree and grow towards the earth. At the ends of the roots are feathery tendrils—making the end look rather like the tail of a cow or the tangled end of an uncombed plait. After the root touches the ground, it enters the earth, tethering the tree.

The root then begins to thicken and widen into a thick woody trunk. Over time, a single tree can spread horizontally over a vast area covering several acres, looking like it is composed of multiple trunks and branches. In reality, the entire tree is one giant entity whose weight is supported by multiple aerial roots that act similar to the supporting beams or columns we use to build our houses. With old trees, it is sometimes impossible to tell which trunk is the parent and which are the clonal offspring that began their lives as roots. A tip passed on by one of our grandmothers is to add banyan roots to hair oil for better hair growth. If you do, she said, your hair will never stop growing, just like the roots of the banyan tree.

Interestingly enough, the banyan is also a favourite of bonsai specialists who find its root system very amenable to pruning. As the aerial roots grow and thicken, they are bent into preferred shapes using wires and other supports. The Kaiyuan monastery in the coastal Taiwanese city of Tainan has a banyan bonsai that is over 250 years old.

Sacred to Hindus and Buddhists, and revered and protected across Indian cities, the banyan is also a tree of paradox. A life-giving keystone species that supports diverse species, the tree also acts as a strangler fig, an epiphyte that grows on and surrounds its host tree, often killing it.

Despite being one of the largest trees in the world, the banyan can also begin life as an epiphyte, in tiny spaces of refuge on other trees. Fruit-eating birds eat the banyan fruits or figs. When they excrete, the birds drop the seeds into a crevice of another tree, or a fork between two branches. The banyan sprouts in such seemingly unfavourable contexts, exploiting any rotting leaves or other material that may have fallen in this crack or crevice to support its early growth.

The seed begins life as a commensal, tagging along on the main host tree. But as the seedling grows into a young tree, its aerial roots begin to surround the host, 'strangling it' as they dig their way greedily into the soil. The leaves form a thick canopy that grows over the host tree, thus robbing it of light from above and sustenance from below. Starved of food and squeezed from all sides, the host tree eventually dies, leaving the banyan—called a strangler fig for obvious reasons—thriving. Other ficus species such as the peepul can also become strangler figs, but the banyan is one of the most common species that does this. This is an evolutionary trick that enables fig trees to grow tall and grab the light from the host, as light is necessary for tree survival, but very difficult to get in tropical forests where these trees evolved.

It is not just other trees that the banyans have taken over. In humid coastal places like Goa, and in cities such as Mumbai and Kolkata, it is common to see banyan trees (and their close cousins, the peepul) sprouting in the crevices of old houses. Left unchecked, these trees eventually take over the house, flourishing exuberantly in decaying urban heritage homes and giving majestic old bungalows an exotic look of a *bhoot* bungalow (haunted house), most popular in Indian movies where ghosts play a central role. Add to this the poignant fact that many Indian freedom fighters were executed by public hanging under banyan trees and it is clear why this majestic tree, which has witnessed events both heroic and tragic, is India's national tree.

The banyan is a favourite of poets and prophets, storytellers and myth-makers worldwide. Some say the tree that Alexander saw is the same as Kabir's banyan. According to local legends, this massive tree grew from the toothbrush of the fifteenth-century mystic poet Kabir, which he tossed aside after use. Kabir's banyan on Kabirwad Island in Bharuch, in the middle of the Narmada river, is said to have once covered an area close to 17,000 square metres and was so large that it could shelter 10,000 horses. If it is indeed Alexander's tree, as it seems likely from the location described by his companions, it is far older than Kabir. The truth of its origins is lost in the shifting sands of history. But we know more about the history of some other famous banyans.

The city of Vadodara is named after the banyan, while the township of Auroville was founded under a banyan tree. Bal Samand palace in Jodhpur has a giant banyan with a big colony of fruit bats. It is believed to be 550 years old. Adyar in Chennai has a 450-year-old banyan tree. A great banyan tree in the Kolkata Botanical Gardens and the Big Banyan Tree of Bengaluru are other centuries-old heritage trees that have witnessed many changes in their surroundings.

Thimmamma Marrimmanu in Andhra Pradesh, believed to be close to 600 years old, is considered the largest banyan in the world, spreading over 19,000 square metres. The tree is worshipped by couples praying for a child. Just to give you an idea of what the size of the tree means—20,000 people can gather comfortably under the shade of this one tree. In fact, thousands of people collect under this tree during its *jatra* (annual festival). Pliny was right in saying that entire troops of horsemen could be concealed under a single tree's branches.

These historic banyans have witnessed our changing pasts and have been commemorated in poems ranging from Milton's *Paradise Lost*, to Rabindranath Tagore's *The Crescent Moon*. If they could speak, they would have much to narrate. The *Brahma Purana* pays tribute to the remarkable capacity of an immortal banyan tree, the Akshaya Vata, to survive the *pralaya* (the great flood). The sage Markandeya, says the *Brahma Purana*, found a banyan tree surviving in the midst of devastation, where he was blessed with the sight of Vishnu as a baby. The Akshaya Vata is believed to be located variously in Allahabad, Varanasi and Gaya. An Akshaya Vata in Allahabad is found at the confluence of the Ganga and Yamuna. The tree is so old that it was described by Hiuen Tsang, the Chinese pilgrim who visited India over 1000 years ago. It is now housed inside the Allahabad Fort and protected by the Indian Army, but visited by thousands of pilgrims during the famous Kumbh Mela.

In more recent times in Mumbai, a large banyan in Horniman Circle, in the old Fort area, has played witness to a fast-changing economic and cultural landscape. The tree has witnessed the transformation of Bombay from a rustic scene with grazing cattle to an urban landscape with British gardens, and later to the bustling skyscrapers of modern Mumbai. In 1855, twelve Indian cotton merchants got together to found the iconic Bombay Stock Exchange under this tree. The stock exchange later moved to another banyan tree, on the nearby Meadows Street. Now considered the world's fastest-trading stock exchange, valued at over 2.3 trillion dollars, who would think that it began under a simple banyan tree?

Banyan (*Ficus benghalensis*)

Description: Full-grown trees have a majestic, dense canopy with aerial roots that drop to the ground and develop into trunks. Bark is relatively smooth, greyish-brown in colour and can appear silvery.

Flowers: Not visible as they are tiny and enclosed inside the fruit (fig).

Fruits: Figs are spherical in shape, downy and turn red on ripening.

Leaves: Oval-shaped leaves with a leathery texture.

Seasonality: Semi-evergreen tree for the most part but does shed leaves in March and April. Fresh leaves are translucent in a beautiful rosy colour. Figs ripen through the year at intervals — fruiting period varies between trees.

Family: Moraceae. Plants of this family contain a milky latex.

Origin and distribution: Native to India and found throughout the country in its cities, villages and forests.

'The Banyan Tree' from *The Crescent Moon* by Rabindranath Tagore

O you shaggy-headed banyan tree standing on the bank of the pond,

have you forgotten the little child, like the birds that have nested in your branches and left you?

Do you not remember how he sat at the window and wondered at the tangle of your roots and plunged underground?

The women would come to fill their jars in the pond, and your huge black shadow would wriggle on the water like sleep struggling to wake up.

Sunlight danced on the ripples like restless tiny shuttles weaving golden tapestry.

Two ducks swam by the weedy margin above their shadows, and the child would sit still and think.

He longed to be the wind and blow through your resting branches,

to be your shadow and lengthen with the day on the water,

to be a bird and perch on your topmost twig,

and to float like those ducks among the weeds and shadows.

FIVE

TALKING
TO TREES

Unlike animals, trees and plants don't move around. We often think that they are not as interesting to observe as animals. Certainly, we may never think of talking to a tree, or even consider that trees can talk to one another.

But in 1983, David Rhoades and Gordon Orians (scientists at the University of Washington) while studying the Sitka willow, observed something that turned our ideas of plant communication upside down. When the leaves of one tree were attacked by caterpillars, the tree responded by making the leaves more unpalatable, filling them with poisonous chemicals. This made sense. Surprisingly, neighbouring trees more than 3 metres away, which were not attacked, also reacted in the same way. This observation was astonishing. It suggested that neighbouring trees received warning signals of some kind from the tree under attack. Other scientists working on other tree species, such as the poplar and the sugar maple, also found evidence of similar signalling.

At first, there was a lot of positive 'buzz' around the idea that trees could communicate. But later, many influential scientists criticized these studies as being anthropomorphic — falsely attributing ideas of human emotion to trees. The criticism was so severe that the main discoverer, Rhoades, had to quit the field of science altogether. The idea of talking trees was dismissed for several years.

Several years later, a number of research studies conclusively showed that Rhoades was correct. Wounded trees could indeed communicate with each other. They did this through signals sent through the air. When the leaves of one tree (or plant) were attacked and eaten, it released a cloud of chemicals into the air. Other trees nearby sensed these chemicals and were alerted to danger. One of the most dramatic pieces of evidence came from Transvaal, South Africa, where an African scientist, Wouter Van Hoven, was studying the unexplained mass death of kudu, the African antelopes. The kudu grazed heavily on acacia trees during a prolonged drought and the trees were in danger of dying. The trees that were overgrazed began to emit puffs of ethylene, warning other trees located at an average distance of 45 metres! All the acacia trees in the area ramped up the tannin production in their leaves, which was harmful for the kudus. The group response by the acacia trees led to the mass death of over 300 antelopes, poisoned by the increased tannins in the leaves.

Is this kind of communication intentional or accidental? Some scientists suggest that trees may be producing volatile chemicals like ethylene to quickly signal to their own leaves. The fact that their neighbours also pick up the signals may be unintentional. Tree neighbours may in fact be eavesdropping on private communications. But chemical signalling does not take place only in the air. Trees also communicate via their roots, sending chemicals out into the soil. Here, the evidence seems clearer that trees are intentionally talking to other trees.

In 1997, while studying the forests of British Columbia for her PhD thesis, Suzanne Simard made a discovery that revolutionized our understanding of tree communication. Trees of two different species — Douglas fir and paper birch — were in constant conversation, even though they were hundreds of metres away. These trees sent messages to each other via an underground network of fungal threads, or mycelia, which connected roots of different trees. During the summer, paper birch trees produced more food than the fir trees, which were in the shade of these larger trees. During the hot months, the birch trees sent food to the fir trees via the mycelial network. In the winter, the birch trees lost their leaves and could no longer photosynthesize food. Fir trees, which retained their needle-like leaves, not only generated food, but also passed on some of it back to the birch trees. Meanwhile, in a 'you scratch my back, I'll scratch yours' network of mutual benefit, the fungus networks also benefited — they were sustained by the food sources that they passed on from one tree to another.

Using this network, which some scientists have dubbed the Wood Wide Web, trees were able to support each other during times of plenty and periods of stress. If one tree was being attacked by a pest, it sent signals to other trees to increase production of 'natural pesticides' to repel attacks. When a tree was damaged, leaving it less capable of making its own food, other trees sent it food through this underground network.

Trees know if their neighbours are kin, that is genetically related family members. They tend to offer greater support to related individuals, creating familial support networks of mothers, daughters and granddaughters. But trees also cooperate outside the family. Trees of different species talk to each other and take care of each other, as the research of Simard and her colleagues has shown.

Especially relevant for us in cities, research on forests shows that 'mother' trees — the oldest trees in a region — are essential for the survival of the entire community. These trees are connected to all other trees. When they are cut down, other trees send food to them via the underground fungal network, keeping them alive for decades after they have been cut. In forests in Germany, tree stumps cut over 500 years back have been observed to be alive, even though they lack branches and leaves, all because their neighbours are sustaining them.

Plants and trees don't just emit chemicals into the air and soil. They also do something more obvious to humans — they produce sounds. We hear the rustling of leaves and the creaking of branches. It is soothing to stand under the shade of a large peepul tree in a busy city area and listen to the constant rustling sound of its leaves. But trees and plants also produce a number of sounds that are inaudible to our ears, at wavelengths that are too low or too high for us to pick up. Now scientists are beginning to suggest that trees may be communicating with other plants, and even animals and insects, via sounds that we may have missed simply because we never thought of it.

Ancient human societies have long believed that people can talk to trees. In ancient Persian, Chinese and Indian mythologies, there are frequent references to the Wakwak or Vagh Vagh tree, which bears fruits that look like human heads. When the fruits ripen, the trees begin to talk, say a number of beloved old fairy tales. Mythologies from Greek to English talk of oracle trees — trees that can predict the future. Alexander the Great was believed to have received a warning from a Wakwak tree of the end of his life and the destruction of his empire. More prosaically, forest tribes may also be using trees to communicate with each other. The Waorani tribe, in the forests of the Amazon, uses the buttress roots of giant ceibo trees to communicate across great distances. The roots produce a booming sound when thumped, much like a subwoofer in a sound system. This low-frequency sound travels across long distances in the forest, helping people find each other when separated. Many other forest communities have independently discovered the usefulness of buttresses. The Jarawa, an indigenous community that lives deep inside the forests of the Andaman Islands, also use buttress roots (of other species, for example species of *Terminalia* and the false hemp tree) to communicate when they are out of sight, and to warn others of danger.

Much has been made of humans communing with trees in cities as well. Several city gardeners talk to their trees and plants, firmly believing that this helps them grow. People even play music to their plants depending on their own preferences. Anecdotes seem to suggest that plants prefer classical, soothing music — whether Western, Indian or Chinese. Music with harsh sounds or strong beats, like rock music, seems to be counterproductive, making plants grow even more slowly. But research studies are still inconclusive. Nobody has been able to establish whether, or how, talking to trees helps in their growth, let alone tell us once and for all what kind of music they like.

But this does not deter a growing number of tree whisperers from cities across the world, who have launched initiatives to get people more connected with nature. Tree whisperers in cities like Bengaluru conduct open-air workshops at tree festivals, getting people to take off their shoes and socks, walk barefoot on the grass with their eyes closed, walk up to a tree and place their bare feet on the roots, later taking their feet up to the bark. With their eyes closed, how does the bare soil feel? And the grass? The bark? Psychologists say that hugging a tree reduces stress. Similarly, while we all love to admire trees, closing our eyes to focus on the sounds they make and feeling their bark and leaves with our hands, feet, arms and legs get us to commune with them in a completely different way.

Biologist David George Haskell has written extensively on his experience in talking to trees. His latest book, *The Songs of Trees: Stories from Nature's Great Connectors*, describes a year he spent with twelve different trees around the world, from Israel to Ecuador to New York. He describes how different species make sounds that are very characteristic. A balsam fir hisses in the wind, while the stiff, needle-shaped bristles of a pine tree generate an intense noise. Attaching ultrasound sensors and microphones to trees, he shows us how trees become noisier on summer afternoons, as the sun's overhead heat dries out their sap, breaking the long water columns inside the tree core, creating a number of little 'clicks and fizzles'.

There are a number of puzzles that still remain about trees in cities though. For instance, when we plant trees in a row along a street, can they create new connections between their root systems? Do fungal networks develop below the soil, if concrete and tar surfaces are laid on top? We need new research to help us answer these questions.

As yet, no one has studied the science of tree communication in cities. What messages does this research on tree communication hold for trees in cities? In many Indian cities, large trees are cut because they are 'over mature', a term that many foresters use to justify chopping old trees. Planners speak of replacing these massive giants with young saplings. But if these trees are more than individuals and are in fact central nodes that support entire communities of trees, we are impacting the future survival of city trees in ways we have not thought of. We should focus on protecting the giant heritage trees left in our cities, as they help to sustain a network of trees near them. Finally, beyond the physical and ecological, how does this research help us develop a different imagination of trees? Is a city with trees, any sort of trees, desirable? Many people relate to trees as species, often based on their childhood memories of playing under one kind of tree and plucking fruits from or climbing another. One large tree may be as good as another if we do not know its name or identity. But people also have an affinity for specific species — some like the amaltas for its spectacular blossoms, while others have a belief that the neem tree is good because it purifies the air.

Going beyond this, can we relate to trees as individuals with whom we develop a special affinity? Many people do this for sacred trees. A peepul tree in a local temple, or a date palm in a favourite much-visited dargah takes us into a mood of contemplation of a higher power. In cities, we may have memories of a favourite mango tree in our grandmother's backyard. A tree on whose branches we spent summer days with a pile of unripe mangoes, a bowl of salt and chilli powder, and a good book — only to be dosed with a spoon of castor oil at night. The famous American poetess Marianne Moore was deeply attached to a Camperdown elm tree in a park in Brooklyn, New York. In her eighties, she wrote a poem to the tree, 'The Camperdown Elm', which inspired a local group to protect this tree and other heritage trees in the park.

We have millions of trees in our cities. Can we develop a similar affinity for them? There are millions of us as well, of course. So perhaps we can, if we begin to recognize each tree as an individual, taking the time to talk to them — and listen to the wisdom they offer us in return. The group events that tree whisperers conduct help city dwellers get in touch with their inner green spirit through touching, tasting, smelling and feeling trees. These innovative approaches are much needed to help us understand what trees are saying. If we learn how to communicate with trees in multiple ways, through science and through imagination, we can also learn how to protect our city trees from the threats of urban stress that are all around them.

SIX

PALMS:
SUPERSTARS
OR HAS-BEENS?

Indian cities are going through rapid changes in their preferences for trees. Moving away from trees such as mango, wild badam and silk cotton, many cities have begun to favour palms. Pretty as a picture, gracefully swaying palms add to the visual beauty of landscapes. From high-end apartment complexes to information technology (IT) campuses and city parks, exotic palms have become the new global superstars, assiduously courted and planted in cities as far apart as Chandigarh, Mumbai and Bengaluru. Where does our fascination for exotic palms come from?

The view of palms brings to mind images of sunny beaches. They symbolize luxury, leisure, and the idea of living life king-size on a coastal resort, with a drink in hand. Palms are also a symbol of southern California, where so many Indians participated in the IT boom of the 1990s. These palms were imported from Mexico and the Mediterranean, and popularized in the gardens of wealthy residents across California in the early 1900s. They were brought in for their decorative looks. They did not provide

51

shade, much needed in the hot semi-arid desert landscape of southern California, nor did they provide edible fruit, or any other useful products. But the association with the tropics and the Mediterranean, and the very fact that these were exotic trees, reinforced the idea of southern California as a place of glamour and entertainment. In fact, the very attributes that made the palm purely ornamental — the lack of messy fruit, spreading roots and large branches — made it a favourite with city officials, who found it easy to plant and maintain this tree on major roads.

In the first decade of the millennium, a number of Indians returned from various parts of the United States of America (USA), where they worked in the IT sector. They brought with them a preference for palms, which they associated with ideas of progress and upmarket living. Many IT companies also landscaped their campuses with palms, aiming to give their employees and foreign visitors a great visual experience. Palms quickly became widespread in luxury hotels, beach resorts, airports and gated layouts across large Indian cities. California imported palms from the tropics to get the exotic tropical climate look — India prefers to import palms from exotic foreign tropical locales to get the chic California look. And there we go around in circles, each location copying foreign trends to look cool rather than looking towards its own flora and what suits its native climate.

A popular favourite is the royal palm, imported to many Indian cities in the past two decades. Pradip Krishen memorably describes it as 'in danger of becoming a bit of a cliché', so widespread is it in Delhi. This palm, a native of Central America and the Caribbean, is regal-looking as its name implies, with a smooth greyish trunk that bulges out midway, slimming down at both ends. Many residential layouts and apartment complexes built in the recent decades have marketed themselves around the royal palm, to the extent of having the word 'palm' in the suffix or prefix of their names. The palm is also a favourite of the technology and financial hubs that are springing up in cities across India. The glass-fronted buildings in these hubs that reflect the glare of the sun on a hot day also reflect the line of neatly planted royal palms. But people rarely pause to stand under the tree as it offers no shade.

Another popular ornamental is the fishtail palm, which gets its name from the shape of its leaves that spread out and resemble the serrated tail of a fish. The palm is indeed aesthetically appealing, especially during the flowering season when bunches cascade down from the crown. Commonly found in Indian forests, the fishtail palm also has a range of uses as medicine, food and as a source of an alcoholic drink. However, in cities it usually serves only decorative purposes. This palm is also steadily disappearing across many regions, though it is preserved in some locations such as *kaavu*s (sacred groves) in the town of Thrissur (Kerala).

There are around 2600 species of palms (from the family Arecaceae) found across the world — some are climbers, others shrubs and stemless plants, and still others, like the royal palm and the coconut, are woody. India has a wide range of native palms, including the palmyra and the date palm. Most palms are found in warm tropical climates, but a few are also found in deserts and warm temperate areas. In the pre-industrial era, three families of plants — palms, cereal grasses and legumes — were believed to be of most use to humans, providing a number of products. Through time immemorial, wild palms have been carefully selected, domesticated and propagated for human use.

The date palm, cultivated in the hot deserts of Mesopotamia in the fifth millennium BC, enabled human expansion across the Middle East. It is no surprise that palms are mentioned a number of times in the sacred texts of the old world, the Bible and the Koran.

In ancient Greece and Rome, palm branches were symbols of victory, handed out in public to winning athletes and victorious warriors. In Christianity, the palm is associated with Palm Sunday, a week before Easter, commemorating the day that Jesus entered Jerusalem before the Last Supper.

Palms are considered sacred in India as well. They are especially worshipped in Tamil Nadu, where the palmyra is also the state tree. Palms were royal emblems, used to crown kings. Panaiveriyamman, a Tamil tree goddess named after *panai* (palmyra), was worshipped for fertility. Palm leaves are used as thatch roofing for huts, the *nongu* (fleshy fruits) are eaten with relish, the sap is drunk fresh as *neera* (palm nectar) or fermented as toddy and palm sugar is used in cooking. The fibre is used to weave cots and make baskets, and the wood to build homes. The ancient Tamil poem 'Tala Vilasam', attributed to the eighth century CE, describes a mind-boggling 801 uses of the palmyra. Some scholars believe that palm leaves were the earliest materials used for writing in Sanskrit. In India, the leaves of the palmyra and talipot palm were in widespread use. Though writing on palm leaves is now largely a lost art in India, tens of thousands of manuscripts survive in various archives. Several of these are palm leaf books, which consist of a number of leaves bound together by a string, and are still used by fortune tellers.

Palms were once a characteristic feature of the Indian coastline. For colonial visitors arriving from the cold shores of European countries, the sight of palms was the first thing that greeted them as their ships steamed into the Indian harbours. R.G. Wallace, in his 1824 memoir, wrote, 'The coast on which Madras stands is lashed by a raging surf, over which the city appears to great advantage, and the numerous palms in its vicinity look charmingly green.'

Writing about Mumbai, James Douglas spoke of a palmyra tree 'shooting up seventy or eighty feet high, the last of a family-group which once stood together and are laid down in the oldest charts of Bombay harbor, and which of yore gladdened the hearts of our sea-sick progenitors'.

One of the most ubiquitous of palms, domesticated for its many uses and found in cities across India, is the coconut. Although the coconut has become such an integral part of Indian villages and cities, there has been much controversy about its origin. Some botanists believe the tree originated in South America, others think that it came from southern Asia. Most now believe that the coconut originated in Malesia, the region between Australasia and South East Asia. As humans moved across the region, they helped in the spread of the coconut, helping colonize a number of islands in the Pacific. Thus the coconut became a part of the food culture of many tropical countries, not just India.

In fact, the use of the word 'nut' is a misnomer. The coconut is, in fact, a drupe—a fleshy or pulpy one-seeded fruit enclosed inside a hard stony covering, which is why drupes are also called stoned fruits. Wild coconuts were long, with a thick husk and shell, and very little water—a fruit that floated easily and spread across islands and coasts. Today's domesticated coconut is of course adapted to human needs—it is much rounder, with a thinner shell and husk, and contains more water. 'Cocos' means 'monkey face', as to the early Spanish and Portuguese explorers who named the coconut, the three black dots on the nut resembled the face of a monkey. The Filipinos call it the 'tree of life' or 'tree of heaven', while in Indonesia it is the 'tree of abundance' or the 'three generations tree', and in Malay it is the 'tree of thousand uses'.

George Herbert, the priest and poet, described the many uses of the coconut in his poem 'Providence':

Sometimes thou dost divide thy gifts to man,
Sometimes unite. The Indian nut alone
Is clothing, meat and trencher, drink and can
Boat, cable, sail and needle, all in one.

Given these myriad uses, for us in India, the coconut is the *sriphala* (the fruit of Sri, the goddess of prosperity). Despite coming from distant lands, the coconut has become an auspicious symbol, important for rituals across the country. One of the most common of Hindu religious symbols is the coconut placed on the mouth of a pot and decorated with mango leaves. Coastal communities especially revere the fruit. The fishing communities in Mumbai celebrate Nariyal Purnima. They offer coconuts to the sea god, seeking protection from untoward incidents, cook a variety of dishes with coconut, have competitions that involve breaking coconuts and plant coconut trees on this auspicious day. Similar festivals have been described in other coastal towns such as Porbandar.

Coconut water, milk and the pulp are all ingredients in cooking. We often stop by coconut sellers with their carts in cities to quench our thirst on a hot summer day. Coconut water has proved to be life-saving in more dire situations too. During WWII, coconut water, believed to be sterile, was intravenously administered to wounded soldiers suffering from blood loss in the absence of the availability of blood plasma.

Across the oceans, the coconut has been adopted for cooking in unique ways. In the 1820s, coconut oil began to be exported from Sri Lanka to England and was used to make soaps. Those who bake are familiar with margarine, developed and promoted during the reign of Napoleon III as an affordable substitute for butter for the poor. By the end of the nineteenth century, the coconut also found its way into the making of margarine. Milk from the dairies of Britain were mixed with coconut fat. This margarine melted in the mouth and was tastier compared to the traditionally used ingredients of animal fat and tallow. Before WWI began, the coconut had established itself as the most important source of vegetable oil in the world, used to make candles, soaps and explosives — essential items in times of war. The demand for coconut oil was so vast that all regions of the world where coconut could thrive had been planted with the palm. The British experimented with other parts of the tree as well. In the book *Culinary Jottings for Madras*, written in the 1880s, a British officer said that if the young white stalks of the coconut flower could be steamed and covered with melted butter, they could be served exactly like asparagus.

Apart from countryside plantations, coconut has also been a popular tree in many Indian cities, flourishing even in poor-quality soil. A second century CE cave inscription in Nashik talks of the grant of 32,000 coconut trees in a village north of Thane. Coconuts were planted on a large scale by the second century, so in all likelihood they must have been introduced much earlier. Soon, the palm had spread across the region. By the eighteenth century, Mahim, today a densely populated neighbourhood in Mumbai, was said to have as many as 70,000 coconut trees. The coconut was taxed, so it also gave income to the British government. In the early 1900s, over 1,00,000 coconuts and other palms were grown in an area covering 870 acres in Mumbai.

But the coconut is very much a tree of southern India as well. The root of its name in the languages of Kannada, Malayalam,

Tamil and Telugu is *ten* (south). Hence the coconut is called *tenkai* (nut of the south) and the tree the *tengimara* (tree belonging to the south). Groves of coconuts were scattered across coastal towns in southern India. Bengaluru was once called a metropolis of monkeys, with the native settlements dominated by the spiky coconut, populated by bonnet macaques, who climbed the trees to feast on the nuts with dexterity. The coconut is believed to be a lucky tree, bringing prosperity to those who plant it in their homes. There is a saying that the coconut palm is as good as an earning son for a poor, retired man. In cities where space is a luxury, trees are often axed to build or extend homes. But the coconut is often spared. Houses and shops in Bengaluru make space for the coconut tree, incorporating them into the design, where they can be seen growing through balconies and garages. The 1970s master plan of Chennai encouraged the planting of coconut orchards in a green belt around the city, with the idea of watering them using the city's waste water.

While the royal palm and other ornamental palms grow in popularity, many Indian and naturalized species of palm such as the palmyra, date palm and coconut are now being slowly squeezed out of cities. Once found in many small towns and cities, especially coastal and southern cities like Kanyakumari and Madurai, these palms were an important part of local diets and livelihoods. However, with modern concrete homes, the replacement of local drinks by bottled soft drinks and the advent of processed cane sugar, local palms are no longer as valued as they used to be. They are now being felled in high numbers.

Ironically, many American cities, from New York to Los Angeles and Miami are beginning to move away from ornamental palms, while Indian cities continue to be obsessed by them. Palms are not ideal for semi-arid cities. The inside of the palm appears more like a grass than a tree, with soft spongy wood. Much of the weight of the tree is water. They grow fast, but transpire at high rates, placing a high demand on groundwater. The canopy covers a relatively small area in proportion to the height. Thus, palm canopies are less capable of providing important ecosystem services such as shade and the cleaning of polluted air. Also, many ornamental palms require regular maintenance to remove fronds, which becomes increasingly expensive and difficult as they grow taller.

Also, exotic palms are often not deep-rooted enough to sustain the dizzy heights to which they grow, especially given the poor quality of most urban soils. Thus, after a few decades they become susceptible to falling in storms, causing substantial damage. Local palms, while they may be subject to many of the same constraints, provide many valuable benefits that outweigh the costs. Planting purely ornamental varieties of palm is a fad that is not only useless but possibly harmful as well, in cities plagued by heat islands, polluted air and depleting groundwater.

As a woman traveller to India, Anne Katherine Elwood, eloquently described 'the tall and airy cocoa, either singly dancing aloft in the air, or presenting, en masse, a continuous shade, the stems resembling the pillars of a gothic cathedral must always be interesting and nothing can exceed the beauty of the more youthful ones, just throwing out its branchy leaves, with a grateful coquettish air, like a young belle in the pride of her charms, claiming, and ready to receive the homage of mankind, to her light and wavy elegance'. It would be a pity if we could no longer find space in the city for the coconut, the date palm and the palmyra, the original superstars, whose fruit and fronds have been so intertwined with our daily lives and histories for centuries.

Palms (*Cocos nucifera* and *Roystonea regia*)

Description: Tall with greyish barks. Royal palm trunk is smooth with a faint bulge. Coconut palms are of different types from dwarf to tall, but all have a rough, ringed bark.

Flowers: Both have creamish-yellow flowers. Royal palm flowers are tiny in dense bunches within a sheath. Flowers of the coconut are larger and more easily visible.

Fruits: Royal palms have pea-sized fruits, green at first that turn reddish. Coconut is a fibrous drupe ovoid or ellipsoid in shape.

Leaves: Leaves are known as fronds, appearing as large, thick feathery extensions at the tip of the trunk.

Seasonality: Evergreen.

Family: Arecaceae. Fruits in this family are usually drupes.

Origin and distribution: Both are not native. Royal palm was introduced from Cuba while coconut comes from Malesia. Coconut is more widespread; cultivated and planted across the country. Royal palm is planted for ornamental purposes.

Riddles and Proverbs about the Coconut

Riddles:

Indian
1. He has three eyes but is not Shiva, he has long tresses but is not a hermit, perches at the top of a tree but is not a bird, gives milk but is not a cow.

Hawaiian
1. Three walls and you reach water.
2. My sweet-water spring suspended in air.

Proverbs:

Hindi
1. *Nariyal mein paani, nahin jante khatta ki meetha* (Water inside the coconut; no way of knowing if it is sour or sweet) refers to an unpredictable or doubtful situation.
2. *Bandar ke haath mein nariyal* (A coconut in the hands of a monkey) refers to a fool who doesn't understand the importance of a good discovery.

Malayalam
1. *Chirattayil vellam urumbinu samudram* (A coconut shell with water can seem as vast as the ocean to an ant), meaning that depending on your needs, what is insufficient for some can be plenty for others.

Konkani

1. *Ordhea maddar choddun hat soddche nhoi* (Don't let go after climbing half-way up the coconut tree). It means you shouldn't leave a job half-done.

Barbados

1. 'Coconuts do not grow upon pumpkin vines', which means that children will turn out like their parents.

Folk Tale about How the Coconut Got Its Trunk

Many of us have heard of the mythological story of Trishanku, the ruler of Ayodhya. There is an alternative folk version of the story, which describes how the coconut tree was formed. King Trishanku was seized by the desire to go to heaven alive. He sought the help of many sages, all of whom refused to help. Finally, the powerful sage Vishwamitra agreed to help him, by conducting a yagna. As the rituals proceeded, Trishanku's body began to rise towards heaven. But the gods, who would not accept this unusual route of approach, complained to Indra, who pushed him down. Pushed up by Vishwamitra and pushed down by Indra, the unfortunate Trishanku remained suspended for a while. Tired of holding him up with his magic powers, Vishwamitra propped him up with a long pole. The pole became the trunk of the coconut. Trishanku's head is the fruit or the coconut. The fibre around the shell is his beard. When you remove it, you can see his face looking at you, with two black spots on top that are his eyes and a third black spot below that is his mouth.

SEVEN

FUN
WITH TREES
IN ART AND PLAY

Before the advent of television and the Internet, school summer vacations were a time for playing amidst nature. Trees were a treasure trove of material. Different parts of trees — seeds and pods, flowers and leaves — were used in games and in craft.

A common tree that is part of most games is the gulmohar, whose flowers and pods can provide hours of entertainment. The tree is also called the mayflower because it flowers in May, at the start of the summer. Each scarlet flower is surrounded by a ring of oval green sepals, just outside the petals. The sepals are red on the upper surface and light green on the underside. A favourite pastime for children is to peel the thin reddish layer away from the green underside of the sepal. If you do this carefully, the red top layer peels off at the base, exposing the gummy side. You can stick the gummy underside on to your fingernails. They make your nails look like fierce claws, green on top, scarlet tipped talons below, taking the place of long nails that children are not allowed to grow at school.

The fruits or pods of the gulmohar are thick and blackish-brown. They are long, growing as much as a foot in length. You can paint on the pods using acrylic paints. The best way to paint these is to use geometric patterns in bright colours, which you can then stack on your bookshelves or on a table against the wall for maximum effect. Other trees have fruits of different shapes that you can paint on. Most of us have used pine cones during school art and craft sessions. When you can't find pine cones, cones from the spiky casuarina trees found everywhere in our cities make for a good substitute. There are many other trees we can turn to — such as the strange capsule-like fruit of the big-leaved mahogany and the round fruit of the wood apple and Buddha coconut.

Tamarind seeds have been traditionally used in games that tested skills of dexterity, concentration and mathematics. They are used not just in India but also in Africa and South East Asia. *Ei sok*, a game played in Thailand where children scoop up tamarind seeds using a paper cone helps children develop skills of coordination and movement. In India, we have a similar game called *uffangali* (seed-blowing game). The equipment required is simple — a pile of tamarind or other seeds, a smooth surface and lots of friends. The game involves collecting all the seeds into a pile and then blowing hard to scatter them. The seeds that are blown away from the pile belong to that player.

In Uganda, tamarind seeds are used as counters in a traditional board game called *omweso*. Similarly, in India, *pallanguzhi* is played using tamarind seeds. A solitary version of this game is said to have been played by Sita to pass her time while she was held captive by Ravana. The game needs two players and consists of a rectangular board of wood or stone with two rows of seven hollows each. Seeds are transferred from hollow to hollow, with complicated rules that dictate when to stop, and when and how to collect seeds. Pallanguzhi is a game of chance, but it also helps in developing counting skills, logical thinking and hand–eye coordination. Today there is a huge push to revive traditional games such as *aadu huli aata* (goats and tigers, a game similar to ludo), *paramapada* (similar to snakes and ladders), *pagade* and *chowka bara*. The English versions of these games are bought from stores or ordered online. But none of this is really needed. All we require is to be able to draw the board on the floor with chalk or rangoli powder, collect tamarind seeds or other hard seeds from the nearest tree during the fruiting season and start playing.

Seeds make lovely decorative items. The red sandalwood or red sanders tree bears gorgeous, shiny red seeds. These seeds can be found in many temples in Kerala, where they are stored in giant *uruli*s (traditional bronze bowl-shaped vessels) at the front of the temple. These seeds are very popular with children, who collect them in heaps and store them in bottles and bowls at home, using them as coins in various games. They are also used to make jewellery and craft items by drilling a hole through them and stringing them on wires. The seeds of the red sandalwood tree remain bright despite age and only fade when immersed in water. Traditional Indian jewellers used these beads as weights to measure gold, with each seed weighing around 4 grams. These small scarlet seeds were popular well beyond the confines of homes in India, making it all the way to Bond Street, London. Here, they were used in fashion jewellery in the 1920s, with the seeds set in gold to make rings, necklaces and brooches, starting a fashion trend.

Other seeds are also used to make jewellery, both cosmetic and religious. In 1891, British traveller W.S. Caine described a visit to the markets of Pune city, where artisans could be found, 'making lovely sham jewellery of some sort of perfumed composition; bracelets, necklaces, chains and anklets of various seeds'. These seeds included the 'red seeds of the rukta chandan, the mottled seed of the betel net, and the deeply furrowed seeds of the rudraksh'. Not much has changed in the 130 years since this visit. Similar jewellery is sold in shops even today, especially in temple towns across India.

The subabul is a fast-growing species with a tendency to turn invasive. A good way of ensuring that its seeds are not dispersed is to make jewellery from them. The Indian mast tree is another common city tree, planted along the boundary of offices and parks. If we strip away the outer covering of the seeds of this tree, the pale white seeds look very pretty. These are also strung together with colourful beads to make necklaces.

If jewellery bores you, bubbles will certainly catch your attention. The soapnut tree is well known in India. Its fruit is used as a hair wash and conditioner, and as an eco-friendly detergent to wash delicate clothes and saris. For children, the fruit can provide an endless source of enjoyment for blowing soap bubbles. All it takes is a soapnut fruit and a safety pin. Stick the end of the safety pin that has the rounded loop into the ripening fruit. Pull it out gently — a thin film of soap appears. Blowing on this can generate bubbles, small in size but beautiful, with iridescent, shimmering blue – green colours, definitely eco-friendlier than the plastic bubble maker sold in shops, filled with harsh commercial detergents.

Another fun tree is the African tulip tree, also called the squirt tree or syringe tree. The flower buds contain a watery liquid. Children collect the buds and squeeze them, squirting the liquid on one another. In north India, for obvious reasons, this tree is called the *pichkari*, after the water pistol used to spray colours during the festival of Holi. In Karnataka, the tree gets the earthy name of *ucche kai mara* (pee fruit tree) in Kannada.

The place we grow up in also influences what trees we have access to. A common game called *marakothi* (tree monkey) in south India has children climbing a tree. One child holds a stick in his hand and climbs up, trying to touch another child. When he succeeds, he throws the stick down. The child he has touched has to climb down and collect the stick. It is now his or her turn to climb up and catch another child. Sword fights using sticks are other fun ways to pass time. A more complex game is *guldoria*, played by flinging hooked sticks between children. The idea is to keep the stick constantly in the air— the game is lost when one player fumbles and the stick falls on the ground.

In south India, the coconut tree is an important source for games. The fronds of coconut leaves are used to make balls, whistles, watches, a dancing girl that moves her hands, and other toys. Working with and weaving coconut leaves requires practice, but it's like riding a bicycle—once learnt, you never forget. The midrib of the leaflets of the coconut fronds are commonly bunched together and sold as broomsticks. But these can also be dried and put to several other uses. These sticks can be used to make bows and arrows. The sticks break often and the arrows hardly ever pierce anything, nor do they go too far. But children can spend many hours honing their skills making bows and using the arrows for safe target practice. Coconut sticks are also used with paper and glue to make kites at home—another favourite activity around the time of the harvest festival Makar Sankranti, when kites are flown from rooftops and grassy plains across the city.

Children love tossing a ball around, but this can become an expensive pastime. Balls get into neighbours' compounds and are lost in drains or on treetops. The fruit of the rain tree is a handy replacement. Smash the pods on the ground using a hard stone, take out the sticky black pulp and shape this into a ball. This, however, must be done quickly before the pulp hardens into a rock-like object. If you are not careful, it can leave an indelible stain on your hands and clothes — and the 'ball' is so hard that it can hurt if it strikes you. Yet this is a favourite with children, used for cricket and throwball. The flower of the rain tree looks like a powder puff and is a favourite with little children playing imaginary dress-up.

With a little bit of imagination there are so many ways to be creative using the different parts of trees growing around us. Handling seeds, leaves, flowers and fruits is a great way of connecting with nature, for adults and children alike. Such memories, built during childhood, stay with us through adulthood. They can provide the lifelong connect that helps us take an interest in nurturing trees around us, in the cities where we make our homes.

Painting on Peepul Leaves

Painting on the skeleton of peepul leaves is an ancient art form believed to have originated in Kerala. It requires patience and time to prepare the leaf skeleton. First, look for a peepul tree near your house and pluck a few green leaves. The best time to collect the leaves (and stock up for the whole year) is in spring when new leaves grow. Choose leaves that are not mature, but not too tender either. If they are mature, they take too long to prepare. If they are tender, they are fragile and easily destroyed during the preparation process.

Take the leaves and place them in a large bowl of water or a wide-mouthed bottle, making sure they are completely soaked. Change the water every other day, gently scrubbing off the top slimy layer with your fingers and adding fresh water. Over time, soaking the leaves will remove the outer covering. In about twenty to thirty days, this covering will begin to fall off in parts, revealing the delicate, beautiful skeleton (midrib and veins). Continue the process until all the green material has fallen off and the leaf skeleton is exposed. Dry the leaves well. Place a coloured sheet under the leaf and paint with oil or acrylic paints. You can paint an elaborate work of art if you are in the mood or just some fun stripes using many colours.

EIGHT

TAMARIND:
THE **FIRANGI**
INDICA

Heroes come in different forms, even in the shape of trees. The city of Hyderabad suffered a devastating flood on 28 September 1908. After a heavy monsoon, a tropical cyclone resulted in the Musi river overflowing. The flood killed 15,000 people and destroyed 19,000 homes. The death count could have been even higher. A massive tamarind tree in Afzal Park, adjacent to Osmania General Hospital, saved as many as 150 people who climbed on to it. Several of those who survived by clinging on to the tree were patients and their relatives from Afzalgunj Hospital, which had caved in because of the floods. The tree, believed to be 300 years old, still stands today. Commemorative events to remember the victims of the Musi flood continue to be held under the shade of this tamarind.

Tamarind trees can tell many tales of adventure and intrigue. In 2004, it was under the shade of a tamarind-lined avenue on Akbar Road in New Delhi that agitators collected to put pressure on Sonia Gandhi to take up the post of prime minister after the

Congress's election victory. One protester is said to have climbed a tamarind tree, refusing to come down unless his demand was met. Even after the issue was resolved, with Sonia Gandhi saying no to the post of prime minister and the crowd finally accepting her decision, a few men continued to perch on the trees.

This unlikely hero is so much a part of Indian culture, particularly Indian food, that many of us will be surprised to find out it is a firangi (a foreign import). The scientific name of the tamarind is *Tamarindus indica*. The name 'indica' leads to the common misconception that the tree originated in India. But in this, the tree has us fooled. It came not from India, but from far-off central Africa, where it was called the 'tree of life'. The tamarind made its way to India millenniums ago. Wood charcoal analysis shows us that the tamarind was found in Narhan, in the Ganga valley, by 1300 BC, and also in the pre/early Harappan period in Haryana. The *Brahma Samhita* scriptures, dating back to between 1200 BC and 200 BC, also talk of the tamarind. Down south, a copper plate inscription of 819 AD mentions a tamarind tree named Mahamadhu — perhaps a tree with large beehives? We will probably never know, but it is fun to speculate.

There are a number of tales about the tamarind from different parts of India. One legend from Sambalpur says that there was a fight between Bhasmasura, the asura chief, and Mahadev (Shiva). Bhasmasura hid in the tamarind tree, but Mahadev opened his third eye. The magical power from his third eye shattered the leaves of the tamarind tree, making them small forever. In Tamil Nadu, the Perumal temple in Alwar Thirunagiri commemorates Nammalwar, one of the twelve famous Alwar saints. As an infant, he is said to have crawled into a hole in a tamarind tree and meditated for twelve years. A massive tree within the temple walls is believed to be the same one—its bark has been stripped away by devotees who believe that it has magical healing properties. The tree bears flowers, but it is said that its fruits do not mature and, unlike other tamarinds, its leaves do not close at night either. Thus, it gets the name *urunga puli* (the tamarind tree that does not sleep).

The Arabs, who had trade relations with India as early as 600 AD, loved the tree as much as we do in India. They gave it the name *Tamar-i-Hind* (date fruit of India) because of the brown fruit that resembled dates. It is believed that the species name, 'indica', was given by Linnaeus, from this derivation in Arabic. The Arabs traded in the fruit, taking it to European and Arabian countries.

The genus *Tamarindus* has only one species—the tamarind that we all know. The tree is never really without leaves, though during the dry season it may be scantily covered. But it looks most beautiful when fresh, tender leaves appear with the onset of the monsoon. We don't usually pay attention to its flowers, which are quite tiny and a pretty creamish-yellow. There is a very interesting behaviour that the leaves display. If you look carefully, you will see the leaves are open during the day, but fold as soon as the sun sets. This behaviour fascinated Alexander the Great and his team. Androsthenes, a Greek admiral who was sent by Alexander on military expeditions, recorded this strange movement of the leaves of a tamarind on the island of Tylos, which we now know as Bahrain, in the fourth century BC.

Many flowering plants show similar behaviour—their leaves or flowers close at night and reopen in the sunlight, a phenomenon with the long and complicated name of nyctinasty. At the bottom of the compound leaf of the small tamarind lies an even tinier organ called the pulvinus. Water rushes in and out of different parts of the pulvinus at dawn and sunset, leading to small changes in pressure at the bottom of the leaf, which press it closed at night, opening it again at dawn. We know how the tamarind closes its leaves (well, at least partially. The chemical details, however, are still not fully known to scientists). But why does it go to all this effort? This still remains a mystery, despite science having progressed in the millenniums since Alexander's great march.

We may not know why the tamarind sleeps at night. But (and perhaps more to the point) we do know how to use it. Almost every part of the tamarind tree has some value. The sour fruits are high in calcium and can be made into pickles or chutneys. Ripe tamarind pulp is of course widely used in Indian cooking, in a variety of dishes. Some communities also use the flowers. In Latin America, the ripe pulp is sweetened with sugar and made into a popular local drink called tamarindo. The British use the pulp to make their famous Worcestershire sauce. But the fruits and flowers are not used in festivals or ceremonies as they are considered too sour to be auspicious. The acidic pulp is much in demand in homes, used to clean tarnished brass, bronze and silver vessels (as well as much valued idols and lamps). The tree's tender leaves are rich in vitamin C and very tasty—they can be made into chutneys, added to sambar, or chopped into chapatti batter. Mangaloreans even have a traditional recipe for roasted tamarind seeds (*pulinkote*), eaten after removing the hard coat. Be careful if you try this at home—this requires strong teeth and you may crack yours if you are not careful.

The seeds have other traditional uses. In Tamil Nadu, a folk performance called *koothu*, performed by the Kaniyan community, uses drums called *makudam*. These drums are made by pasting leather to a wooden frame, using glue made from tamarind seeds. In Bengal, a powder made from the seeds is used by master craftsmen, who mix these with powdered colours at very high temperatures and use the resulting varnish and colours to paint idols. Over the years, the artisans had shifted to using commercial paint. But in recent years, the famous craftsmen of Kumortuli in Kolkata have returned to using home-made dyes with the help of tamarind seeds. Not only are these cheaper, they are also longer-lasting and eco-friendly. Tamarind wood has its uses too. It is termite-resistant and hardy, and sought-after in cities as fuel. It can be used to make furniture as well, and charcoal produced from the wood can be used to make gunpowder. The wood was once used as fuel for gasogens or wood gas units, which converted wood or charcoal into gas, and powered Indian vehicles during WWII.

In its original home of central Africa, the tamarind occurs naturally in dry savanna woodlands. The Senegalese capital, Dakar, is named after the local name for tamarind which is *dakhar*. But the tree has now spread across the world and is grown in fifty-four countries. Not surprisingly, India is the world's largest producer of tamarind. One of the oldest man-made tamarind groves is the Nallur Amarai grove, close to the international airport in Bengaluru. This is a massive grove of trees, covering a little over 53 acres. Some of the trees are believed to have been planted during the reign of the Chola dynasty, several hundred years ago. The grove was protected by special watchers appointed by the British government, who also planted additional trees here. In 1887, the grove had fifty-five big and 342 large tamarind trees, and provided a source of revenue for Bengaluru. It now has over 300 trees. Carbon dating has found that the oldest tree here is over 400 years old. The old trees have a unique feature. They bear prop roots, which look like that of the banyan — roots that emerge from the trunk to provide support. These suckers enable the tree to spread, allowing new canopies to sprout from the parent plant.

The Nallur Amarai grove is famous across India. It is the first biodiversity heritage site to be declared in the country. Sadly, the grove is now somewhat neglected, overgrown with weeds, with unregulated grazing by livestock that nibble on the leaves and threaten the trees. Garbage is dumped in the grove as well, especially during temple fairs, and by weekend revellers from the city who do not know about or appreciate the ecological and historical significance of this centuries-old grove.

The tamarind has been a popular roadside tree for centuries. It flourishes on dusty roadsides, thrives in the heat, provides shade and acts as a windbreak in windy areas. The small compound leaves are efficient at collecting dust particles from the air and at reducing noise pollution. The tree was a favourite with the Mughal rulers. Babur, who established the Mughal Empire in India, described the tamarind as a 'very good-looking tree, giving dense shade' in *Babur Nama*. In Akbar's time, the fruit (called *ambli*) was economically valued and sold in the market.

Tamarind trees were planted by the Mughals in cemeteries and mausoleums, and around settlements. A particularly iconic tree was planted at the tomb of Tansen (the incomparable musician who formed a key part of Emperor Akbar's court) in Gwalior, visited by musicians who wished to pay homage. This was a double-edged blessing. James Forbes, in *Oriental Memoirs*, wrote in 1834, 'His tomb was formerly shaded by a spreading tamarind tree, which has been so often stripped of its leaves, bark, and tender branches, by these musical votaries, that it is now almost a sapless trunk, in the last stage of decay. A chief reason for this spoil is the prevailing idea that a decoction from the bark, leaves, and wood of this tree, gives a clearness and melody to the voice.'

Sher Shah Suri and Jahangir planted trees along Grant Trunk Road, favouring a mix of the tamarind and mango, to provide shade and fruit to weary travellers. The nawabs of Avadh also planted the tree along main roads in their kingdom. In a village in Bijapur, an 890-year-old tamarind tree planted during the time of King Adil Shah still survives. Tamarind groves were described in sixteenth century Mumbai, beyond the Gateway of India, in the foreshore of the beach, under which fishing nets were strung. In the 1750s, a tamarind tree stood near the city's St Thomas Cathedral. Under the shade of this tree, auctions of cotton were conducted. The hack carriage drivers referred to this place as the *amli agal* (in front of the tamarind). This tree no longer survives, having been cut down in November 1846.

H.F.C. Cleghorn, considered to be the founder of forest conservancy in India, strongly urged the then government of Madras to plant the tamarind as an avenue tree in Chennai in 1860. Red tamarind trees were also planted in colonial Ahmedabad, on the roads leading up to Kankaria Lake. In Delhi, tamarind was one of the trees that helped in the greening of the colonial city in the 1820s, thriving where others failed to take root.

Tamarinds were once found across south India. Many of these trees have been lost to road expansion. But their memories remain. Thus, Puliyanthope (tamarind orchard) is today a congested locality in the city of Chennai, but must once have been a green oasis. Chinchpokli, a suburb in south Mumbai is named after the tamarind trees (*chinch* in Marathi means tamarind) that were once found in abundance. Near many lakes in Bengaluru and other south Indian cities, it is common to find a solitary tamarind tree at the bund. At the base of the tree, a series of small stones are often worshipped, symbolizing Shiva and his sisters. Some communities in Gujarat and Maharashtra believe the tree to be sacred, worshipping the tamarind once a year, on Amli Agiyaras day. Many Indians, however, are averse to sleeping under the tree at night, believing that it is inhabited by ghosts.

It is rare to see tamarind planted along the streets these days. One reason, often given, is that its pulpy fruits make the roads sticky when vehicles run over them. It is a pity to let such considerations influence planting. We cannot allow the tamarind to disappear from our streets. This firangi indica, a staple in our diet and a hero in times of crisis, deserves better.

Tamarind (*Tamarindus indica*)

Description: Large tree with spreading branches and dome-shaped shady crown. Bark is dark brown to greyish-brown and cracked.

Flowers: In clusters, pale yellow and red. Buds are pinkish-red.

Fruits: Long, slightly curved pods, flat but bulging over the seeds. Initially green, then covered with a light brown shell that turns dark and brittle as the fruit ripens. Sticky, brown pulp surrounds the dark brown seeds inside matured pods.

Leaves: Feathery leaflets, small in size and rounded.

Seasonality: Some differences across regions. Evergreen to semi-evergreen tree. Where it sheds leaves, it does so in February, with the fresh leaves, light green in colour, appearing in March and April. Flowering can begin in April and extend into August or later. Fruiting is normally ten to eleven months after flowering.

Family: Fabaceae. Seeds in this family look like beans.

Origin and distribution: Native to tropical Africa, now naturalized in India and found across the warmer regions of the country.

Seed Shapes of Tamarind

How would you describe the shape of a tamarind seed? Well, it can be a tongue-twister if we try to be very exact. Different seeds can be described as being elliptic, oblong, rhombic, ovate, obovate, obtrullate or angular obovate, triangular, or obtriangular and cuneate. But within each there are sub categories, as many as thirty in all. For example, the seed can also be depressed obtrullate or depressed angular obovate. The next time you look at a tamarind seed do have a go at describing it.

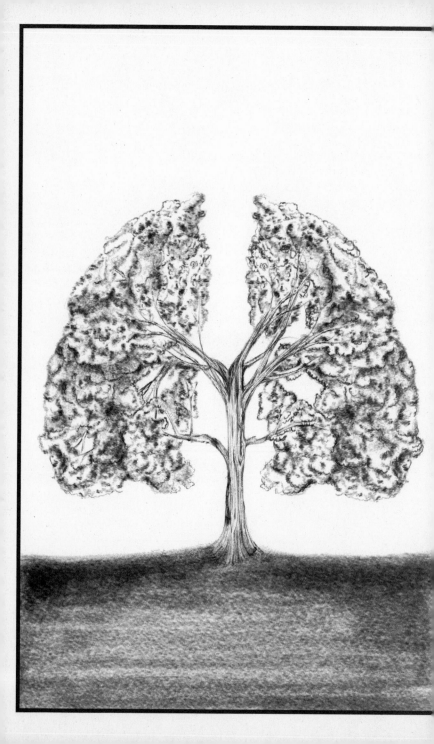

NINE

TREES
AND THE
ENVIRONMENT

There are heated debates about the need for trees in cities. Some people feel that trees in cities are a nuisance, offering a number of reasons. The leaves and ripe fruits that fall on the roads and on parked vehicles are messy and difficult to clean. Trees also take up space on pavements used by pedestrians and block street lights at night. They fall during storms and heavy rain, disrupt traffic causing electricity breakdowns and damaging vehicles, resulting in injury and even deaths.

Do cities need trees? Many argue that they are a luxury. While it is nice to have tree-lined roads and parks in developed countries, it is difficult to accommodate them in growing Indian cities. But trees are a daily necessity in every city. Without their presence, life in the city would be impossible. Trees are essential lungs for the city, providing oxygen, taking in carbon dioxide, filtering and cleaning polluted air. In hot Indian cities, trees also contribute shade and cool air. They help recharge ground water and sequester carbon. Trees are important for the poorest of the poor, providing fruit, oil, grazing material and firewood. In the heart of the city, they offer sacred spaces and places of contemplation, providing relief from stress. Trees in cities are not just a luxury, but an essential part of a healthy environment.

Every summer, newspapers and television shows are full of concerns about the rising temperatures in cities and towns. A constant refrain is how cool the city once was. Each summer, old-timers in garden cities such as Bengaluru and hill towns such as Dehradun and Shimla nostalgically remember a time when homes did not even have fans. Today, not only are there fans in every room, but many homes have air conditioners and coolers too. Instead of maidans and trees, cities are covered with concrete, asphalt, gravel, slate, shale, bitumen, tar and tiles, absorbing heat throughout the day. Congested buildings and tall apartments block the wind and trap hot air.

The trapped heat makes the temperature in cities several degrees higher than its surrounding countryside. Our cities have become heat bubbles, a phenomenon called the urban heat island. In the years to come, heat waves will become increasingly common because of climate change and urban heat islands. Reports warn that many people may lose their lives to heat strokes and suffer from diseases. The worst affected would be those who labour in the open and vulnerable sections of the populations like the sick, elderly and young children.

This is one of the (many) reasons why we need trees in the city.

Urban heat island effects can make the simple act of walking on a city road unbearable. One of our studies conducted in Bengaluru some years ago clearly shows the difference that trees can make. In roads shaded by trees, air temperature ranged from 23.1 to 34.2°C. In nearby stretches of the same roads — barren of trees — the temperature was 3 to 5°C hotter. Road asphalt heats up much more under the sun, of course. The temperature of the road surface reduced by as much as 27.5°C due to the shade from trees. The cooling effect of trees is very important for those who walk and cycle on city roads and wait at the side for a bus. Without trees to protect us from the sun, walking on roads would be like walking on a frying pan. Street vendors know this well. In the afternoon, you can see most vendors searching for shade to protect themselves as well as the fruit, vegetables, clothes or DVDs that they sell. Trees cool the air by screening the road from the rays of the sun. Trees also transpire, letting out moisture from their leaves that cools the air in the same way that we sweat to cool our skin. Offices and homes can reduce their air-conditioning bills and their medicine costs by planting trees within 100 meters of their windows.

The British, who found the searing temperatures in the Indian subcontinent difficult to live in, knew this well. In Mysuru, a memo to the officiating secretary to the then chief commissioner of Mysore, dated 7 January 1876, specified that 'avenue trees are not grown for the sake of timber. The first requisite is that they should provide a maximum of shade without impeding traffic.' A forest officer in 1941 was aghast at an order to cut down babul trees on a highway to get firewood to feed the road rollers, calling it 'sheer vandalism'. Shade and cooling were important motivations for the British to plant along roads. In doing so, they were only following in the footsteps of early rulers such as the Marathas and the Mughals, and Tipu Sultan — all of whom were known to have planted trees on roadsides to provide shade and fruit for weary travellers and marching armies.

Further back in history, during the third century BC, Emperor Ashoka planted banyan and mango trees, and dug wells along the

Royal Road (built by his grandfather Chandragupta Maurya) 'for the comfort of cattle and men'. Sher Shah Suri planted large fruit-bearing and shade-giving trees along sections of the Grand Trunk Road, a practice continued by Mughal emperors such as Jahangir. In north India, roadside trees were considered important along major highways, as they shielded passers-by from the hot summer winds, or 'loo' as it is commonly called, which blow across the Gangetic Plains in the summer, and the cold winds that blow in winter. The winds brought dust that choked the caravans on the road and the extreme heat cracked the road. Trees on the roadsides protected the passengers as well as the road itself. In the Mysuru region, local legend says that Hyder Ali built *kattes* (platforms with large shade-giving trees) at half-day distances from markets, so that travellers and merchants could seek shelter from the midday sun and then continue on their way. Many of these kattes survive across Mysuru and Bengaluru even today.

The air we breathe in cities is loaded with pollutants and fine particles that cause allergies, bronchitis and even death. Nearly 1.2 million deaths are estimated to have been caused by air pollution in India in 2017. For those who think in terms of gross domestic product (GDP), air pollution results in a loss of 3 per cent GDP. The air we breathe has sulphur, nitrogen dioxide and fine particulate matter that enters our respiratory system and literally clogs our lungs. Size matters — the smaller the particles, the deadlier they are when we inhale them. Northern India has one of the highest concentrations of fine particulate matter, a fact obvious to any resident of New Delhi, for example, who dreads the smog and smoke-filled winters. Cardiovascular and lung-related diseases are on the rise in cities in India. Breathing gases such as sulphur dioxide causes irritation in the nose and throat, and respiratory problems such as wheezing, coughing and shortness of breath.

Trees can help reduce air pollution, though they cannot remove it entirely. They help remove fine particles from the air, which are deposited on the hairy or waxy surfaces of leaves. Our study in Bengaluru showed that street trees significantly reduce suspended particulate matter and sulphur dioxide levels.

Tree planting, however, requires some care and there cannot be a one-size-fits-all planting scheme that will work across all cities. The climatic condition of each city needs to be kept in mind to understand what species would thrive there. Social factors also matter. In Bengaluru, congested residential neighbourhoods require narrow-canopied trees like the drumstick and Indian beech while the highways are better served by trees with majestic canopies like the rain tree.

In general, trees with large leaves and dense canopies have more surface area and can absorb more particulate matter. Trees with a rough surface, with hairs or ridges, are better at tackling air pollution. Care should be taken while planting trees though. Since tall buildings already block wind, trees should be planted in places where they help the breeze along, instead of blocking it further. This is particularly important along roadsides. A continuous canopy of trees on both sides of the road can cause a tunnelling effect, trapping polluted air on the road. One way to address this is by leaving small gaps between canopies and to prune the trees, leaving slits to allow the air to escape. Trees are best planted for their anti-pollution effects in places frequented by vulnerable sections of the populations — near schools and hospitals, for example.

Of course, an evergreen tree has additional advantages in a place with hot climate compared to a deciduous tree, as the leaves can absorb pollution throughout the year. But in northern Indian cities, which are hot in the summer but cold in the winter, a careful selection of deciduous trees would work better. During the summer, the tree can provide shade while in the winters, when the leaves fall, the bare branches can allow for much-needed sunlight to filter in.

The mango is not just the king of fruits. Green belts of mango work well in industrial areas with highly polluted air. Ficus trees like the peepul, banyan and Mysore fig thrive in polluted cities, as do the golden amaltas, pink cassia, and the red African tulip and palash trees. Neem, guava and jamun are moderately tolerant to air pollution and are easy to plant and maintain along roadsides. The tamarind, with its compound leaves, is a good tree to plant at dusty or smog-filled locations like intersections. Trees with a large canopy, such as species of ficus, mango, copper pod and rain tree provide much-needed shade and are excellent as avenue and park trees. But we need to make sure that we avoid trees that generate a lot of pollen, as this can exacerbate respiratory allergies.

Trees can also protect cities from the effects of droughts and floods. The roots absorb and hold water, helping rainwater percolate into the ground and slowing down the speed of water rushing over concrete. But today, many city trees seem strangled by concrete paving right around the base of the trunk, leaving no room for the water to trickle down. It is a wonder that these trees survive, despite decades of neglect and active destruction.

While trees are clearly important for survival in cities, their own resilience is tested in the direst of situations. The Bhopal gas tragedy, an industrial disaster whose impacts continue to be felt even today, did not spare trees either. Neem and peepul were one of the worst affected, with loss of foliage and burnt leaves, while mango, eucalyptus and Indian mast tree were relatively unaffected. But in two months, even the worst-affected peepul and neem trees, which had completely lost their leaves, sprung out fresh leaves. This says something about their resilience.

Cities are polluted by more than just dust and smog—the constant noise of traffic, construction and honking can drive anyone mad. Robert Frost in his poem 'The Sound of Trees' asked:

I wonder about the trees.
Why do we wish to bear
Forever the noise of these
More than another noise
So close to our dwelling place?

Frost was talking about the sound made by the rustling of leaves and tree branches. The sound of wind blowing through leaves is a pleasant noise, soothing to our senses. This noise acts as white noise, muffling other unpleasant city sounds such as the honking of vehicles and screeching of tyres. Trees also provide a habitat for birds and squirrels whose chirps and songs provide a pleasant distraction from daily stresses. The soothing rustle of leaves ensures that at the end of the day our nerves are less frayed and our tempers are more even.

There can be many strategies to address pollution and rising temperatures in cities. We can develop new kinds of construction materials, paint roofs white and insist on advanced, less polluting technologies for cars and factories. Bizarre initiatives spring up in the news, such as installing massive towers to suck in polluted air, spraying water cannons from helicopters and burning thousands of kilogrammes of mango wood as part of prayers to reduce pollution. In this obsessive search for miracles, whether God-given or provided by technology, we fail to consider one of the best, low-tech and cost-effective solutions around. We must plant and nurture trees that help reduce heat and pollution, in addition to the range of other benefits they offer to people and biodiversity.

TEN

THE GREAT
EUCALYPTUS
DEBATE

If you are holding a copy of this book, the paper on which these words are printed may have come from a eucalyptus plantation. Apart from paper, eucalyptus wood is used for packaging and making paper boards. The raw material used for newsprint, and well, the reams and reams of tissues and toilet paper we use nowadays are all dependent on this common tree.

The genus *Eucalyptus* is part of the botanical family of myrtles (Myrtaceae). All members of this family of evergreen species have leathery leaves that contain a large number of oil glands. Some eucalyptus trees also bear flowers with oil glands. Many other trees in the Myrtaceae family, including popular fruiting trees such as jamun and guava, as well as a number of aromatic plants such as the clove, allspice and bay rum also produce aromatic oils used in cooking and as flavouring agents. The oils also have antioxidant and anti-cancer properties, making them very useful in herbal medicines as well as in the design of new drugs.

There are close to 900 species of eucalyptus found across many parts of the world — the vast majority of these originated in Australia. Because they are fast-growing trees that do not require much maintenance and can be sold for a lot of money, commercial eucalyptus plantations have now spread out across the world. After Brazil, India has the largest area under eucalyptus plantations. However, the tree has a chequered history of growth and removal in India.

How the species came to India, and spread out across the world, is a fascinating story. James Cook, the son of a farm labourer, was a British explorer and expert map-maker who made three memorable voyages to various parts of the South Pacific between 1768 and 1776. On his first voyage, he took along Joseph Banks (eventually the director of the famous Royal Botanical Gardens in Kew) and other botanists. Banks and his colleagues collected and described a number of Australian plants, most of which were unknown to Western science until then.

Among these plants were a number of eucalyptus trees. The flowers of the eucalyptus are quite unusual, lending the trees their name. When the flower is still a young bud, the petals join to form a cap-like object that covers the top of the bud. European botanists named the genus *Eucalyptus* from the Greek words 'eu' (well) and 'calyptos' (covered) as a tribute to the unusual bud, enclosed and capped. Just before the bud opens, the cap falls off. What lies within, and looks like petals, is actually a mass of feathery, showy and attractive stamens. Within the stamens lies the pistil, the female reproductive part of the flower. Eucalyptus flowers have an important adaptation that helps to prevent self-pollination. First, the stamens mature and release pollen. At this time, the pistil is still young and immature and cannot receive the pollen. This reduces the likelihood of the flower mating within itself (which would be the worst form of genetic inbreeding one can imagine). Later, once the stamens have matured and released their pollen, the pistil matures, now ready to receive pollen from another flower and begins the cycle of life once again.

Soon after Cook's first voyage to the South Pacific, eucalyptus was growing in Europe. In 1774, a species known as brown top was planted in the Kew Gardens, from seed donated by Captain Tobias Furneaux who was also part of Cook's first voyage. India followed Europe closely in its botanical experimentation with eucalyptus. Tipu Sultan, the famous ruler of Mysuru, introduced eucalyptus to south India in the 1790s. Sixteen different species of the genus were either gifted to Tipu by his French allies, or sourced by him directly from Australia. The trees were planted in Tipu's garden in Nandi Hills and some of these still survive today. Tipu was a keen horticulturalist, bringing in a number of species of economic value from different parts of the world. So his early experimentation with eucalyptus is not surprising. But soon he got involved in the Anglo–Mysore wars with the British and died in 1799, unable to take his ideas forward.

There the matter of the eucalyptus rested in India, for several decades. Meanwhile, the trees were becoming very popular in Europe and its other colonies. Botanists quickly discovered that the tree grew fast and had many uses ranging from timber, fuelwood and paper pulp to oils and honey. An added advantage was the habit it displayed of coppicing. If you cut the tree near its roots, new stems sprung up in a few months. Within a few years a fresh crop of woody trunks was ready for harvesting.

In the 1830s and 1840s, two British military officers Captain Dunn and Captain Cotton introduced another species, the Tasmanian blue gum, in the Nilgiri Hills of Tamil Nadu, to provide a source of fuelwood for the local communities. Many of these trees also persist and can be found on roadsides even today. In 1856, regular plantation of the tree was introduced in the Nilgiris and around the hill station of Ooty. By 1860, a number of experimental plantations of as many as 105 different species of eucalyptus were tried out in north Indian towns such as Agra, Dehradun, Saharanpur, Lucknow and Madhopur. Some of these trees still survive today. However, overall the plantations had mixed success. Other trees became more popular, especially the casuarina, another fast-growing Australian import that was planted across the Nandi Hills.

In the 1950s, a fungus attack devastated the casuarina plantations. Searching for a replacement, eucalyptus seeds were collected from local trees and used to raise new plantations. These seeds most likely came from a hybrid between two species of eucalyptus planted in Tipu's times, mostly blue gum, with some influence of swamp mahogany and perhaps some mixture of river red gum as well. Over generations, this hybrid became naturalized and established itself in the local environment. Called Mysore gum, the naturalized hybrid proved to be very successful in India. It could grow well in the high mountains as well as the low plains, flourished in both cold and hot conditions, and even through drought. Tipu Sultan's original collection of trees, imported in the 1790s, naturalized over centuries in India, have now made their way to different parts of the world, including far-flung countries such as Sudan.

Over the years, India has experimented with close to 170 species and varieties of eucalyptus. Apart from Mysore gum, only four other species have worked well enough to be grown on a large scale — Tasmanian blue gum, lemon-scented gum, rose gum and river red gum. The first two are the species used to make eucalyptus oil, while the others are preferred for paper pulp. So, if you see a eucalyptus tree in your city, it is likely to be one of these five. The most common eucalyptus tree in cities is the blue gum and the Mysore hybrid, which has now spread across most of India. These trees are quite easy to identify because of their pale, peeling barks. Children peel off the bark painting them with acrylic paints and using them as natural materials in art.

In its native country, Australia, the eucalyptus is considered an extremely useful tree, especially by the Aborigines — akin perhaps to what the mahua is to the Adivasi tribes in India. The seeds and powdered roots of some eucalyptus species are used as food by Aborigine people. Gall-inducing scale insects, which are found on many eucalyptus trees in Australia, exude a sugary liquid. They are popularly known as marina and are used by the Aborigines to make sweet drinks. Roots of certain species have the ability to store water. If you make an incision on the root, water bubbles out from the tip — a useful property in times of drought. Aboriginal craftsmen hunt for termite-infested eucalyptus trees, using their hollowed-out trunks to craft didgeridoos (trumpet-like wind instruments). Clearly, the eucalyptus is a much-valued tree that grows without controversy in Australia. But what is its story in India?

There are many reasons for planting eucalyptus in India. For one, it is a fast-growing species — it takes only four to five years for the tree to grow and provide a source of paper pulp. Also, it is an extremely hardy tree that grows well even in drought-prone areas. The essential oils produced by the leaves and stems are noxious to insects and cattle, protecting the saplings and trees from cattle and goats. Thus, many absentee landlords can safely plant eucalyptus in their fields and leave them to grow without much maintenance. The wood burns well, sometimes, too well. If the foliage is not cleared and the dry branches not trimmed and removed, especially in dry forests, fires can spread easily through these plantations during the summer. But this very property makes the wood, and even the leaves, much sought-after in villages for stoking fires in houses.

The British were enamoured with these trees. British rule in India was filled with anxieties about environment and health, especially in cities. They were focused on getting rid of miasma, or bad air, which was believed to be the cause of many diseases. Later, of course, scientific experiments proved that germs caused diseases. However, for most of the nineteenth century, the British believed that the quality of the air was the culprit for malaria, typhoid, cholera, plague and other fevers.

Vapours from marshlands were considered the unseen enemy. One of the most debilitating illnesses the British feared in tropical India was malaria, which killed their men in the hundreds. They believed that planting eucalyptus in the marshes and swamps around settlements could arrest malaria by sucking the marshlands dry. The volatile, scented vapour surrounding the trees, especially in the early mornings, was also believed to be salubrious, warding off miasmas. A letter in the *Madras Mail* of April 1882 says, 'He who introduces a species of Eucalyptus, and proves it hardy in the plain of South India, will deserve to rank not far below those who brought cinchona from the antipodes.' Cinchona is, of course, the tree from which quinine was extracted and used to treat malaria. The British considered eucalyptus as a healing tree with similar medicinal properties, as well as economic benefits, adding both to the health and wealth of the colonial empire.

After Independence, Indian foresters established a number of forest plantations but these did not yield as expected. Government subsidies were then provided to encourage farmers to raise eucalyptus plantations to promote the pulp and paper industry.

The tree became popular with many farmers who moved from labour-intensive crops like paddy and sugar cane to eucalyptus. Two species of eucalyptus, the Tasmanian blue gum and lemon-scented gum, were used to extract eucalyptus oil in local industries. The medicinal properties of the eucalyptus come from a chemical called Eucalyptol, which is extracted from this oil. The oil was much sought-after, used to prepare soaps and insecticides, and added to steaming water to treat colds. The trees were planted along forest edges as windbreaks. Swathes of eucalyptus plantation were spread across India by the 1980s.

Then the tree ran into trouble.

Environmentalists complained that eucalyptus plantations in forests had led to the creation of wildlife deserts. The tree was held responsible for depleting soil moisture. The research is not conclusive and there is no clear evidence that eucalyptus plantations are, say, worse than water-guzzling cotton or sugar cane plantations, which the eucalyptus trees have replaced in many locations. However, they have certainly impacted wildlife and biodiversity in many forests where they were planted after cutting down and destroying the original vegetation. Birds cannot eat their hard seeds and deer and other herbivores cannot tolerate their leaves. The roots and fallen leaves of many eucalyptus trees produce allelopathic chemicals that prevent undergrowth, impacting many species of insects, birds and animals.

There were also undeniable social impacts. Many food crops like rice, corn and millets produce stubble and chaff which can be used to feed cattle and other livestock. Eucalyptus plantations, with their lack of undergrowth, could not support livestock. Since these plantations did not require much maintenance, farm labour was let go. This affected many landless agricultural labourers who lost an important source of income.

The Great Eucalyptus Debate spread across the country. Writers called the eucalyptus plantations that had blanketed the countryside a green desert. Environmentalists argued that we should be planting other species like the native Indian beech, a fast-growing leguminous tree that can help increase the fertility of soils while also providing excellent wood. Mahasweta Devi, the renowned writer and activist, even called for an 'anti-eucalyptus movement on a national scale'. A number of protests took place in villages, with many protesters uprooting eucalyptus seedlings in government plantations and replacing them with tamarind. Karnataka saw some of the most vociferous protests, resulting in a ban on eucalyptus plantations on private land in the state. It is ironical that Karnataka should ban this tree, given that it was first introduced in India in the Nandi Hills, near Bengaluru.

While much of these protests were centred around rural India's concerns, eucalyptus has also faced opposition in cities. The British thought the eucalyptus to be an unsuitable species to plant on city and town roads, as they grow tall and are an obstacle for electricity wires. Old and tall trees were special hazards, causing a lot of damage when they fell during storms. In cities like Bengaluru, the large-scale planting of eucalyptus in the catchment areas of the nearby Arkavathy river over the years has been blamed for the river drying up.

However, eucalyptus was also promoted in many cities. While greening Bengaluru in the 1980s, eucalyptus was identified as one of the best species for creating a green belt around the city. There are towering rows of eucalyptus on either side of the road leading up to Dehradun. The tree was planted on many roadsides, again because of its ability to grow fast and establish itself in poor soils with little need for watering, maintenance or protection from cattle and goats.

Eucalyptus species are unsuited for cities in many ways, though they are found across several. Trees bearing leaves with hairy, sticky or wrinkled surfaces capture more suspended particles from the air than trees with smooth, waxy leaves like most eucalyptus species. The volatile organic compounds emitted by the trees interact with nitrogen oxides emitted by traffic, producing an even more harmful pollutant — ozone — which can cause cancer, impact lungs and lead to heart diseases.

Occasionally though, the tree finds supporters. In 2017, an attempt to fell old eucalyptus trees was met with protests by the residents of Chandigarh, who argued that the trees were a part of the city's cultural heritage. In 2018, a plan to cut close to 3000 trees, most of which were eucalyptus, in Noida (ironically to make way for a biodiversity park), was met with protests. Local residents said that the trees were their lungs, tying rakhis to them and hugging them in a manner inspired by the iconic Chipko movement.

A common accusation against the eucalyptus is that it provides no habitat for biodiversity. But this is not entirely true. Given their impressive heights, they tower over many other trees. Cormorants found around lakes in Bengaluru build their nests on eucalyptus trees and the black kites that feed off the garbage dumps in New Delhi are found in abundance on these trees, which provide a high perch for raptors. The dried branches and lopped twigs are used as firewood by migrant workers in shanties and slums. The steam produced by the fresh leaves, dropped in boiling water, is used by the rich and poor alike in cities, helping ward off colds and allergies, and preventing a few expensive visits to the doctor. The eucalyptus has its uses and its ills.

The Great Eucalyptus Debate continues to rage on. It is a tree with character, disliked and loved in equal measure. The conundrum of the eucalyptus is a challenge that may not be resolved anytime in the near future.

Eucalyptus (*Eucalyptus sp.*)

Description: Diverse genus of trees. Very tall trees, with hanging leaves and generally small-sized canopies. Bark is smooth but the colour can vary. Some species shed bark in strips, exposing the lighter coloured trunk.

Flowers: Can be of different colours depending on species. Usually small and brush-like.

Fruits: Usually woody and cone-shaped.

Leaves: Usually lance-shaped with a waxy surface.

Seasonality: Evergreen, but in the tropics may shed leaves at the end of the dry season.

Family: Myrtaceae. Leaves and stems of this family have aromatic oil glands.

Origin and distribution: Native to Australia, but cultivated across India though not tolerant of very cold climates.

ELEVEN

SACRED
AND VENERABLE

'Because there are trees, we know there are gods.'

An old Hindu priest whose shrine was located near a grove in Bengaluru said this to us. Hindus consider many species of trees to be sacred. The ancient Sanskrit text *Vrukshayurveda* by Surapala tells us about the worship of different trees. Planting trees was an act that earned an individual merit for the afterlife—the kind of blessing depended on the type of tree planted. One who planted banyan trees went to the abode of Shiva, while he who planted mango trees went to the abode of Garuda, for example. Surapala offers a human-centred view of tree plantation. He says that it is better to plant a single tree by the roadside, under which people can rest, rather than several trees in a forest.

Trees are worshipped in many parts of the world, not just in India. Tree worship is found across religions too. Both the Bible and the Koran talk of trees such as the date palm, fig, tamarisk and olive. The twenty-four Jain tirthankaras were associated with a sacred tree each, including many of the trees we see in cities, such as champaka, Ashoka and peepul. Buddha is always associated with the peepul. Early representations of Buddha did not show his form — he was always represented as a tree on monuments. The Egyptians worshipped Goddess Hathor, whom they associated with the sycamore fig. The pharaohs of Egypt were buried with many items to sustain them in the afterlife. Among the things they took to their graves were dried figs, enabling them to call Hathor.

Our reverence for trees continues till this day, even in the heart of our cities. Most obvious are the banyans, peepuls and cluster figs. Ficus species are worshipped across the Indian subcontinent, with kumkum (vermilion) and haldi (turmeric) smeared on the trunks and sacred threads and cloths tied around them. We can see pictures of gods and goddesses, and broken idols which cannot be worshipped, left between the branches or at the base of these sacred trees. The cluster fig, however, is not planted near homes, where it is considered inauspicious.

Other common trees are as sacred to us as the figs. The bilwa (bael) is beloved to Shiva, for instance, and can be found in temples dedicated to him across India. The three-lobed leaf of the bilwa is said to represent his *trishul* (trident). The neem is associated with the goddess of smallpox, Shitala Devi. Mango, tamarind, jamun, coconut and palms are all planted in temples, while Ashoka and peepul trees are found in Buddhist monasteries. Tamarinds and date palms are often seen in mosques and dargahs.

The bidi-leaf tree, a species of *Bauhinia*, is important in festival rituals, especially around Dussehra. *Bauhinia* gets its name from the German botanist siblings of the sixteenth century, John and Casper Bauhin. The leaves of this species of *Bauhinia* have a peculiar shape, with two leaves that join to form a single leaf (like a camel's hoof) that represents the two brothers. In Maharashtra, the leaves of the bidi-leaf tree, known as *apta* or *svet kancha* are exchanged on Vijayadashami. The demand for these leaves is so high that entire trees are sometimes stripped of their leaves. In such cases, city authorities have had to issue orders protecting these trees during the festival season. The champaka, a common street tree in towns and cities in southern India, is revered by Hindus. The tree is planted in temples and its flowers are offered in worship.

Most trees worshipped in India are native species, but this is not always true. A classic exception is the cannonball tree, also known as *naga linga pushpa*, so called because the flower (pushpa) resembles the hood of a snake (naga). The tree made its way from the West Indies or South America to India probably sometime before 1000 CE and was then absorbed into Hindu religious traditions. Interestingly, the tree is not worshipped in its original home.

The frangipani, which came from Peru, is abundant around temples. The flowers are used for daily worship in many homes. The tree is also known as the kalki tree, planted by some Muslims over their graves to act as sentinels. The tree symbolizes immortality owing to its ability to produce flowers and leaves even after being uprooted. Its flowers adorn graves throughout the year. Great power is accorded to the seed of the tree as a cure for bites from the venomous cobra. Folk beliefs claim that the tree has no pods, as the cobras destroy them out of fear.

The baobab is associated with Gorakhnath, a Hindu monk believed to have lived around the eleventh and thirteenth centuries CE and who is said to have preached under the tree. Hence it is sometimes called *gorakh chinch* or *gorakh ambli*. Native to west and central Africa, it is now found along the west coast of India and in the Deccan Plateau. The tree is commonly associated with the rule of the medieval Deccan sultanate. In the Deccan, executions were carried out under the tree, though why it was chosen for this grisly purpose is not really clear. Some say the tree was brought to India between the tenth and fourteenth centuries by Arab or Portuguese traders, while others say it was introduced by African slaves. A massive specimen known as the Hatiyan Ka Jhad (literally the elephant-sized tree) stands in the premises of the Naya Quila fort in Hyderabad. This tree is believed to be the biggest in India, around 475 years old, and is said to have been gifted to Quli Qutub Shah. The massive tree has a hollow trunk that is said to have hidden forty thieves evading royal armies.

A number of old trees are similarly associated with saints. Adi Shankaracharya, the eighth-century philosopher and theologian, is said to have meditated under a mulberry tree in Jyotirmath. Some say this tree is the oldest mulberry in India, more than 1200 years. A khirni tree, said to be the oldest of its kind in New Delhi, stands in the dargah of Hazrat Nasiruddin Mahmud Roshan Chirag Dilli, the last of the Sufi saints of the Chisti order in Delhi. The dargah was built in 1356 CE. The tree is said to have been planted much before. What tales of the past these trees have witnessed and could tell us, if only they could speak.

Less formal than the dargah or the fort are rudimentary shelters of dry branches tied together with twine to protect stones that are worshipped under trees such as mango, jamun, tamarind and ficus, and can be found across cities. In many parts of India and Nepal, raised platforms on which peepul and neem are planted are common. These have different names — *ashwathkatte* in Kannada, *aalthara* in Malayalam and *chauthara* in Nepali. These sacred platforms, often painted in stripes of red and white, can be found on the most congested of roads and in quiet temple compounds. The peepul and the neem, representing male and female trees, are planted alongside each other on these kattes. On auspicious days, a marriage ceremony is performed between the neem and peepul, and newly married couples offer their prayers.

Snake stones are often kept at the base of these trees, donated by infertile couples seeking children. Women visit them, seeking the blessing of the gods by circumambulating the tree and tying threads or red cloth around the peepuls, for instance. But these platforms are also places for social meetings. Sometimes the kattes are just spaces for women to have a few moments to themselves or to engage in conversation with other women, away from the demands of home and families.

Many small towns across India also have sacred groves. The kaavus of Kerala are managed by the government, temple trusts, local community, or even privately. In Thrissur, there are as many as 970 such kaavus in the district, of which 220 are in the heavily populated urban taluk of Thrissur. These kaavus are tiny oases rich in floral and faunal biodiversity, many less than an acre in area. They contain rare trees such as the south Indian kanak champa, which is categorized as vulnerable in the IUCN Red List of Threatened Species. They also host a number of birds, bats, butterflies and insects. While there are presiding deities from mainstream Hinduism in these kaavus, the serpent god is popularly worshipped. Thus many of these groves are called *sarpakaavu* (*sarpa* meaning snake). A visit here can be a soul-stirring experience. To stand amidst the towering trees draped with creepers, allowing little sunlight even at noon, lit by a lone lamp under the snake shrine, can leave anyone with a sense of awe. The character of these kaavus are, however, changing. Some are being used as garbage dumps by city dwellers, while others are converted to modern temple structures with the trees eventually surrounded by concrete or even cut down.

Some trees bring to mind the culture and heritage of an entire region. An example is the chinar in Jammu and Kashmir. The word *chinar* has its origins in Persian and translates into 'what a fire!' It describes the colour of the leaves, which turn red, yellow and amber—the various shades of fire—in autumn. The tree was a favourite of the Mughals who called it *buen*. They declared it to be a royal tree, protected it and planted it across Kashmir in groves and landscaped gardens. The Dogra kings who ruled Kashmir between 1847 and 1947 also protected the tree. The oldest chinar in Kashmir is believed to be over 700 years old. It was planted by the Sufi saint Syed Abdul Qasum Shah. The Hazratbal shrine, within the University of Kashmir campus, also has hundreds of chinar trees around it. Several of the other mosques and shrines in the Kashmir Valley have chinars, as do the temples dedicated to Goddess Bhavani. But the chinar is now threatened in Kashmir. Many trees have been cut down and the remaining are threatened by disease, pollution and road-widening. A ban on cutting them is the only hope for saving this sacred tree.

Like the vanishing memories of the chinar, the memories of the heroes who took part in the Indian freedom struggle are also fading. In the premises of the Sabarmati Ashram in Ahmedabad is a dead neem tree, its white branches stretching towards the sky. This neem was planted over a century ago. Under its shade, Mahatma Gandhi introspected about his internal struggles and the direction the freedom struggle should take. Yet, visitors to the ashram pay attention to the buildings but ignore this tree that has witnessed so much.

Consumed by our harried urban lives, we forget the past. Indian cities have been shaped over the centuries. The ecological landscape in the form of trees is as much a part of their centuries-old history as are the temples, mosques, dargahs and other spaces.

The sacred beliefs that our ancestors associated with nature are important even today, not just because of our religious beliefs, but also because of the awe in which we hold the natural world. We need to reconnect with the heritage value of trees in our cities, for our own survival.

This message is beautifully captured in the Malayalam saying *kaavu vettiyal kulam vattum* (if you cut a grove, the pond will dry). There are strong links between our sacred affinity for trees and the modern, urban way of life. The day that we fail to respect our trees and look at them solely in terms of utility will mark the end of nature in the cities — and perhaps the end of our survival too.

TWELVE

AMALTAS:
GOLDEN
CHANDELIERS
WITH BUZZING BEES

Have you seen the maps of our cities in urban master plans and vision documents? They show increasingly smaller and smaller patches of green, indicating the decreasing spaces for trees. Our cities are turning grey as the built area is increasing. But just by planting flowering trees along city avenues we can transform them into multicoloured places of beauty, and not just on paper. What better colour to include but the gold of the amaltas!

Amaltas is a deciduous tree native to India. The tree is medium-sized and has a spreading, irregular-shaped canopy. It belongs to the legume family and is a relative of the familiar peanut and pea. The tree derives its fame from its spectacular golden blossoms that flower between April and June. The flowers are borne in bunches along both sides of a common stalk. The older flowers are at the base, with the smallest and newest buds at the end. In full bloom, the glorious bunches of golden-coloured flowers look like gracefully bending chandeliers that light up the tree. Sometimes the tree is so covered with flowers that the leaves and branches are completely hidden in a shower of gold. Often, fallen golden petals cover the grass or street below. It is a visual treat. Standing under the tree while the petals shower down upon you is an unforgettable experience. Small wonder that this deciduous forest tree has become a favourite ornamental species exported to different parts of the world, from South Africa to West Indies and from China to Brazil. Amaltas flowers are also edible. They can be made into pakoras or sautéed and ground with coconut and roasted Bengal gram into a chutney.

Amaltas fruit are equally unusual-looking—long cylindrical pipe-like pods. From these pipes comes the scientific name of the tree, *Cassia fistula* (Cassia, or *kassia*, in Greek, indicates that this is an aromatic tree, while 'fistula' in Latin means pipe). The family Fabaceae was described as far back as the first century CE in *De Materia Medica*, the classic five-volume Greek encyclopedia on herbal medicines by physician and botanist Pedanius Dioscorides. The tree has also been used by Arab and Greek doctors to make herbal medicines for centuries. If you open the long pods, you will see a number of seeds inside, separated by sticky pulp. The amaltas is a popular tree across India and has several vernacular names. In Hindi and Bengali it is known as *bandarlathi* (monkey stick), because monkeys are supposed to like the sweet pulp of the pods.

The tree is deeply embedded in Indian culture, from north to south. It is a key indicator of the forest landscape of Sangam literature, associated with romantic imagery of separation and waiting. In the epic *Śilappadikāram*, which dates back to somewhere between the fourth and sixth centuries CE, one of the flutes played by Krishna is said to have been made from the *konrai* or amaltas. Its flowers are believed to be an incarnation of Shiva and are often described as resembling his matted locks. On a survey around

Mysore in 1800, Francis Buchanan found amaltas leaves burnt by the Bayda community, bee collectors, below hives of the rock bee, *Apis dorsata*. The acrid smoke of these leaves, along with those of another plant, drove the bees out of their hives, after which the tribe could safely collect the honey and wax. He also documented the worship of Ganesha in the form of a stake of the tree, cut and placed into the ground. Before sowing seeds, people offered milk and rice to the stake and prayed for the success of their crops.

Amaltas is the national flower of Thailand, as well as the state flower of Kerala. The blossoms are very important for the festivities of Vishu, the Malayali new year. The festival itself is simple and held without much pomp. It is a time for the family to get together in their new clothes, burst a few fireworks at the crack of dawn and enjoy a feast. On this day, the auspicious sight of the *Vishukkani* (*kani* means something you see first in the morning) is believed to bring good fortune. The *konnapoovu* (amaltas flowers) is an essential part of Vishukkani. Without the konnapoovu that blooms during this time of the year, Vishu is incomplete. Keralites who stay in cities where the flower is not accessible substitute it with other yellow flowers. But nothing can match the beauty of the amaltas, which is why some even try to grow it in pots and encourage it to bloom before Vishu.

The amaltas were painted beautifully by Marianne North, a remarkable woman — an artist, naturalist and traveller in the restrictive nineteenth-century Victorian era. Her autobiography, *Recollections of a Happy Life*, recounts her travels across the world, including in India. She describes the amaltas she sees in Lahore, then a part of British India as 'a perfect mass of yellow, with flowers and pods more than a foot long'.

The India Post would seem to agree with North about the beauty of this tree, releasing a number of stamps on the amaltas flowers. The Kerala circle of the India Post released a one-rupee stamp with the amaltas to commemorate the golden jubilee of the formation of the state in 2006. The India Post also released a stamp in 1981, as did the Department of Posts in 2000 and 2011. A special cover with commemorative and regular stamps was also produced by Rafi Ahmed Kidwai National Postal Academy in 2016.

The amaltas is easy to spot in the dry and moist deciduous forests of India. Yet, for a long time, one of the greatest mysteries about the tree was how it reproduced in the wild. The mystery so intrigued a British forest officer, Robert Scott Troup, that he conducted a fascinating experiment at the Forest Research Institute in Dehradun in 1911. Troup collected ripe pods and buried them in two plots, leaving one unprotected and covering the second one with a mesh. Within a week, jackals discovered the pods buried in the unprotected plot. They broke the pods with their teeth to get to the sweetish pulp, scattering the seeds not just in the unprotected plot but also in other parts of the forest through their scat.

Over time, the seeds in the unprotected plot germinated, while those in the protected plot rotted, or were eaten by ants, and did not sprout. Clearly, animals were crucial for the germination. Perhaps the seeds needed to get into the digestive tract and pass out in the scat to be activated. Later research showed that not just jackals, but monkeys, bears and pigs too could help in the spread of the tree. The amaltas that blooms in the Delhi Ridge is thought to have been aided in its spread by jackals.

Artificial reproduction of the seeds is not an easy task, as any of us who have wanted to plant the tree in our gardens have found out. To begin, try extracting the seed from a fallen pod of the amaltas – it is an almost-impossible task as the pod is hard and difficult to break. The seeds too are very hard and may take several months to germinate.

Troup suggested boiling the seeds in water for five minutes to aid early germination. Seeds from older pods germinate more successfully.

The story of its pollination is even more fascinating. The amaltas is pollinated by bees and butterflies, but most pollination is by the carpenter bees (of the *Xylocopa* genus). Over countless generations that stretch way back into history, the carpenter bees and the amaltas flower have evolved together in a most well-matched way. The flower is essential for the bees, providing them with pollen. Similarly, the bee performs an essential service for the flower, as it takes the pollen to another flower to pollinate and fertilize, giving rise to seeds that ensure a new generation of plants. Pollen is essential for bees, which eat this protein-rich food to build their own muscles and use it to feed their larvae. The anthers of the flowers, which are the parts that contain pollen, are connected to small ejecting tubes that are closed at their entrance. These tubes have only a small hole – so small that insects cannot enter. How are they to get at the pollen then?

The bees extract pollen through buzz pollination. Carpenter bees grab the amaltas flower and shake their flight muscles very fast. This produces a loud buzzing sound. The resulting vibrations shake out pollen grains from the flower. The size of the bee and the speed at which it shakes itself determines the frequency of the vibration. Specific flower species have co-evolved with specific bee species, so that, for the amaltas, the specific carpenter bee's frequencies are the ones that dislodge its pollen.

But it's not as simple. The bee and the flower have opposing desires. The bee wants to collect all the pollen and use it as food. But the flower wants the pollen to land on the back of the bee, so that it can fall on to the next flower the bee visits and pollinate it. The flower wins by tricking the bee. Each flower contains different sets of stamens. The set on the top of the flower, which the bee sees first after landing on the flower, contains the pollen meant for it to harvest.

Unknown to the bee, which is busy extracting pollen, focused on the upper rows of stamens, the lower stamens shoot out a jet of pollen. This pollen needs to reach the upper back of the bee, where it cannot see or remove it. Here, it is perfectly positioned to brush against the stigma of the next flower that the bee visits and pollinate it. But there is a catch. How can the pollen from the stamen, located below, reach the upper part of its back? By using an ingenious process of repeated ricochets. The pollen jet shoots out from the anther when the bee shakes itself and hits a petal. The petal that receives the jet of pollen deflects it in another direction (much like a petal would deflect a ray of light). After a couple of ricochets (or more), the pollen jet is finally redirected where it needs to go and lands on the back of the bee. One study, in Brazil, found the bees to be so involved in collecting pollen from the upper stamens of the amaltas that they did not realize that much greater quantities of pollen were being deposited on their backs.

Buzz pollination is a specific adaptation found in approximately one out of every eleven flowering plants, and as many as 15,000–20,000 plant species use this approach. The size of the flower, the location of the petals and the bee are well-matched by generations of co-evolution so that the pollen reaches the exact spot on the bee's back where it needs to go. A true marvel of nature.

Carpenter bees may be specialized pollinators, but they are not the only insects the amaltas supports. The flowers attract a large number of other insects, including bees, but also many butterflies. The leaves also attract other insects. A close inspection of the tree will show weaver ants and fruit flies lurking in the foliage for very different reasons, such as preying and mating: war and love in equal measure.

In Delhi, the amaltas is a common and much-loved species lining several avenues. It was a favourite of the Mughal rulers who planted it in many of their famous gardens. As a nod to this, the iconic movie *Mughal-e-Azam* shows Prince Salim romancing Anarkali in a bower decorated with drooping amaltas chandeliers. The tree is found in Lutyens' Delhi as well. Pradip Krishen, in his inimitable way, says it is, 'in danger of becoming (like the peacock), so common that we stop noticing it'. But the blossoms, as bright as the noon sun, make one pause, even in the hot Delhi summer, to admire the tree's beauty. Even the carpet of golden petals that fall on the roads only to be crushed under treading feet or moving vehicles is a pretty sight. A massive tree at Teen Murti Bhavan, planted by Sanjay Gandhi, is a spectacular sight in summer. This tree is an essential part of India's history, commemorating times when the ashes of Indira Gandhi and Rajiv Gandhi were placed under the tree for visitors to pay their respects.

In the 1900s, amaltas trees were found in many parts of Bombay (now Mumbai). The south Mumbai neighbourhood of Byculla is said to have derived its name from *bhaya-kala* (the level ground of the *bhaya/bawa*, which is the amaltas). The British called it the Indian laburnum. Interestingly, Laburnum Road in south Mumbai also derives its name from the row of amaltas planted during the British times. These trees have now disappeared from the road — having been replaced by *Peltophorum* trees with yellow flowers, but these cannot match the singular glory of the amaltas. Similarly, there was said to have been a beautiful amaltas in the compound of Hotel Spencer in Chennai with a girth of seven feet.

The tree is not just beautiful but also useful. It is known as the *aragvadha* (disease killer) in Ayurveda for its medicinal properties. The pulp that separates the seeds is sweetish and used as a purgative and laxative (a bizarre factoid that does not gel with the gentle beauty of this gorgeous tree). A paste of the root helps with skin diseases and the leaves can help heal ulcers. The colourful flowers can be used as a vegetable dye for fabrics like wool, while the dried and powdered flowers are a natural colour used in Holi.

The wood is hard, used for firewood, agricultural tools and fence posts. The bark produces a red dye that is used in tanning. Because of this property, amaltas was much in demand in British India. In Bengaluru, a letter dated 23 June 1873 describes a request from one Badódṁ Sábi for ten cartloads of the bark of the amaltas, to be used for tanning, at a rate of Rs 2 per cartload.

But not all people are enamoured by the tree. It is considered to be invasive in Queensland, Australia. Closer home, there is a belief among the Gonds that bringing a part of the tree into the house can cause family discord. The Gonds place the seeds of the amaltas in the thatched roof of their enemies' houses. As the seeds in the dried pod rattle in the wind, the residents of the house are believed to become noisy and quarrelsome.

The blossoms of the amaltas have caught the imagination of many poets and writers as well. Ida Colthurst wrote a book on the flowering trees of India in 1926, describing the blossoms of amaltas as 'graceful, tossing plumes of glowing gold'. Sarojini Naidu, freedom fighter and poet, was also enamoured by the blossoms. Her poem 'Golden Cassia' says:

> O brilliant blossoms that strew my way,
> You are only woodland flowers they say.
> But, I sometimes think that perchance you are,
> Fragments of some new-fallen star;
> Or golden lamps for a fairy shrine.
> Or golden pitchers for fairy wine.

No one can remain untouched by the beauty of these golden chandeliers. The spectacular blossoms of the amaltas ensure that the tree finds a special place in any book on flowering trees in India.

Amaltas (*Cassia fistula*)

Description: Medium-sized to small tree with low branches. Smooth yellowish bark that darkens with age and is covered with crusts.

Flowers: Bright yellow, in drooping bunches; older flowers at base and younger ones towards tip.

Fruits: Long cylindrical pipe-like pods, black when mature, very tough to open and enclose seeds in compartments separated by sticky pulp.

Leaves: Leaves shaped like imli (tamarind) — but larger.

Seasonality: Deciduous tree that sheds leaves starting in March and extending into May. The beautiful bright flowers appear in late April and flowering can extend into July or even later. Fruits usually ripen between December and April.

Family: Fabaceae. Seeds in this family look like beans.

Origin and distribution: Native to India and found across the dry and moist deciduous forests of the country.

THIRTEEN

NATIVE AND EXOTIC:
IDENTITY CRISES
OF TREES

For as long as people have lived on this planet, there have been questions of belonging and identity. Reams of newsprint and hours of passionate debate have been devoted to questions of who is 'originally' from a place, and who is an outsider. Perhaps surprisingly, the same debates also rage about the identity of trees. A variety of terms are thrown around — native, exotic, naturalized, invasive. Alien invasive species are ranked alongside deforestation and climate change as one of the biggest threats to biodiversity that the world faces today. But in today's globalized world, does the origin of a tree really matter?

India is well known as a global melting pot of cultures and cuisines. It is also a confluence of biodiversity. Many of the trees that we see in Indian cities came from far-flung corners of the world, including Australia, Brazil, Madagascar, Malaya, Senegal, South America, West Indies and many other locations. Some species like the coconut may have floated in from the sea, passing from island to island and eventually arriving on the Indian coast.

Others like the baobab were brought in by slaves and saints, while traders and travellers brought commercially valuable fruit, spice and timber trees. Some trees, such as the tamarind, were brought into India thousands of years ago, certainly before 1000 BC. Others like the rain tree and copper pod are newer imports, coming into India as recently as the nineteenth and twentieth centuries. Some trees were brought as gifts for kings, or commissioned by kings who were keen botanists and horticulturalists, such as Babur and Tipu.

Colonial botanists built on this tradition, bringing in tree species from their colonies across the world. British, German and Indian horticultural experts planted trees in cities such as Bengaluru, inspired by Kalidasa's famous treatise *Ritusamhara*. Trees were carefully selected so that they blossomed serially. The city looked beautiful at all times of the year, with flowers of different colours in bloom. To do this, they had to look across the world for species. Within one location and one type of habitat, trees evolve to fruit and flower at similar times of the year, adapting to their seasonal and ecological conditions as best as they can. But tree planners in cities can free themselves from such constraints.

City tree-scapes in India are somewhat like paintings, carefully composed by planners and planters from a mixed palette of species from across the world. There is a rich history to these species. If we dig into their origins, we will hear fascinating tales of travellers and traders, merchants, mendicants and rulers who influenced the country. These species, which we refer to as exotics, were brought from distant lands and represent the global influences that have made cities in India what they are today. As with other kinds of global influences, there have also been heated debates about whether exotic trees are a boon or bane. Some writers wax eloquent about the gorgeous visual landscape of cities covered with exotic flowering species. Others complain that native species are slowly disappearing from our urban avenues.

Part of the debate is cultural. Some tree species that we think of as quintessentially Indian in fact arrived as exotics. Over thousands of years, they have become naturalized to the extent that few remember their exotic origins. Classic examples include the tamarind and the coconut. The tamarind has been around in India for thousands of years. Charcoal remains of the tree have been found in pre-Harappan and early Harappan excavations in India, and it is mentioned in ancient Hindu texts too. Indian cooking is unthinkable without the tamarind, which is an integral part of so many recipes. But the fact remains that it is not a native species and, in fact, originated in central Africa.

Fossil records of the coconut have been found in the Indus Valley civilization (3100–2800 BC). The fruit is an essential part of Hindu rituals and ceremonies, and is described in post-Vedic texts, such as the Mahabharata. But the coconut also seems to be exotic. The Indian subcontinent is a secondary centre of origin for the coconut, and while there is still some controversy about its source, most experts believe that it originally came from Malesia, a biogeographic region that includes the Malay Peninsula and the islands of the archipelago.

An Indian landscape is unimaginable without the tamarind and coconut today. But other trees, equally prominent, were introduced by various rulers relatively recently. The Nilgiri Hills were a favourite spot for experimentation with exotic trees. Eucalyptus was brought to India by Tipu Sultan in the mid-eighteenth century. The tree is now a firm favourite of foresters and plantation owners, and is found across India in forests, farmlands and cities. The cinchona tree was smuggled out of Peru by a British explorer and planted in the Nilgiris in 1860, with the aim of combating malaria and breaking the South American monopoly over quinine. The Australian black wattle was brought in more recently, in the 1940s during WWII. Its bark was used to tan leather. Another Australian import, mesquite, was introduced in the nineteenth century in Sindh and Andhra Pradesh to provide fodder and fuel to dry parts of the subcontinent.

Cinchona trees have remained relatively confined to the plantations where they were placed, in part because they were attacked by Indian pests, such as the grub of the cockchafer beetle, and eaten by the Nilgiri sambar, which nibbled down mature trees to sticks in many cases. Eucalyptus, wattle and mesquite, however, thrived and spread beyond the confines of their plantations. These trees have been criticized for being water-hungry exotics. Mesquite and wattle are invasive and have spread into neighbouring forests and grasslands, destroying biodiversity and reducing the water table.

But these trees are not all bad. They have their uses too. Local villages use all three species for firewood, while mesquite also feeds cattle. Many farmers choose to plant eucalyptus and wattle on their plots for a few years. These trees grow fast, provide an assured income and require little maintenance. At the same time, it is also true that they have spread into many adjacent forests and grasslands, completely changing their structure and function, and in many cases, devastating the local ecology and impacting wildlife. In many cases, invasive plants and trees also impact the livelihoods of local people who depend on forest species suppressed by the invasives.

India is not unique in its challenges of dealing with invasive species and exotics. A 2002 study by the Food and Agriculture Organization (FAO) of the United Nations found that 1121 tree species were reported to have been taken from their native place of origin to different parts of the world. Many of these introduced species have become naturalized, integrating into their new environments and cultures. But 442 of these were reported as having become invasive, spreading into and impacting native forest ecosystems. These numbers only describe the species that have been studied and written about by scientists. The actual number of exotics and invasives are likely to be much higher. One of the world's twenty biodiversity targets, laid out by the Convention on Biological Diversity, is to eradicate or control invasive alien species and prevent the introduction and establishment of invasives.

All exotics are not invasive though. Why do some exotic species become naturalized, while others turn invasive? The answer lies in the connection between the tree and the ecosystem that they inhabit. Species such as the Australian acacia are not invasive in their homelands. They grow and thrive in the right soil and weather conditions, but are also checked from growing out of control by natural predators—herbivores that graze on them, insects that feast on the leaves and seeds, and fungal and bacterial infections that infect trees. When these trees are brought into other countries, either by choice or by accident, they usually travel alone, leaving their grazers, insect predators and microbial pests behind. When they reach their new homes, some species are eaten by local cattle and insects, and thus kept in check.

Some exotic trees may never be pollinated or dispersed in their new environments, especially if they require specialized bee or bird species to pass on the pollen or disperse the seeds. These species will always be dependent on humans for survival in their new environments. Other trees may be relatively untouched by pests and predators in their new homes. One example is that of the eucalyptus from Australia in India, whose leaves produce strong-tasting chemicals that keep the cattle and insects away. If exotic trees are wind- or water-dispersed, they can spread easily in new environments too.

These are just some of the factors that influence the spread or control of exotic species. Other traits or characteristics that influence the likelihood of a species to become invasive or naturalized include how deep its roots go in search of water, how fast its fallen leaves decompose, how fast it grows, whether it is taken from place to place by humans and animals, and a number of other factors that the initial introducer may never have thought of. Most countries, now recognizing the dangers of an exotic tree spreading out of control, have put in policies to prevent introductions of foreign plants, trees and animals. (Animals and insects can also be invasive, with equally devastating consequences for local ecology.)

But the danger of exotics, though raised in earlier times as well, did not deter the European colonial empire, which was focused on finding the 'best' location to grow trees from across the world, bringing species from one colony to another. The British were particularly fascinated with South America and the Amazon — lush tropical regimes rich in species they had never seen before. They smuggled the seeds of the rubber plant out of South America, taking it across the world. Some British explorers wistfully said they wished the British had acquired the Amazon instead of India, for the botanical wealth that it possessed. Kew Gardens in London was an important halfway resting house for many of these introduced trees. Seeds and saplings were brought to the gardens, acclimatized and propagated, and then taken to other countries. Many trees and plants moved into India during the British times.

This was a two-way process. Many Indian species were also moved to other locations. There were several reasons for this transfer. The inexhaustible scientific curiosity of the British led them to take plants they had not seen to London, for Linnaean classification and preservation. Plants were valued for their commercial importance, for their beautiful flowers and as sources of food in new colonies. Acclimatization societies were set up across Europe, beginning with France in 1854. Their goal was to encourage the introduction and naturalization of non-native species in different countries. The British also brought many trees from their homeland into the tropics. British oaks and firs were distributed across city cantonments in different parts of India, planted by homesick British officers and their families who sought to feel more at ease in this alien land.

The British obsession for aesthetic landscapes led to the import of a number of exotic trees. We see avenues of gulmohar in many cities. This tree comes from the island of Madagascar. The jacaranda with its pale blue feathery blossoms is native to South America. The horticulturalists were enamoured with flowers, but the native peepul and shisham fell out of favour. Some experts raised warnings, asking for caution in selecting and planting the right exotics in the right place, and stating that native trees needed to be preferred as much as possible. But the preference for new imports continued.

In more recent times, planners and citizens are increasingly beginning to prefer native trees in cities. When heavy rains and cyclones uproot trees, some say that native species survive better, tending to be more deeply rooted. Exotics such as the gulmohar, with their spreading buttress roots, are one of the first to fall in a storm, for instance. But storms may not always make such fine distinctions as we humans do. After Cyclone Vardah lashed Chennai in December 2016, native, exotic and naturalized trees were all uprooted. Gulmohars from Madagascar were felled in the cyclone, but so were the native mango, peepul and banyans, and the naturalized tamarind.

Exotic trees are also criticized for being water guzzlers in cities and draining an already-low water table. Native trees are commonly believed to provide a more suitable habitat for local biodiversity. Some native species like the peepul also have a cultural and religious identity in Indian cities that help protect them from the axe. A rain tree in the same situation may not be as lucky.

Flowering exotics are also preferred by some citizens and urban planners, as the flowers add to the beauty of the landscape. In Chandigarh, the eucalyptus has become a focus of recent controversy. While some want the tree to be cut down because it is water-hungry, others want to save it because it is an integral part of the city's identity. More research needs to be conducted to reach a conclusion on many of these aspects, as the evidence is largely anecdotal, often differing across locations.

Our perceptions of exotics sometimes reflect in the tone we use while referring to them — as if we are speaking of an unwelcome, often villainous, arrival in the neighbourhood. In reality, it is difficult to draw clear lines separating the native from the exotic, especially with naturalized trees that have been around for centuries, even millenniums. Certainly, species like the rain tree and tamarind have integrated with the local ecologies, whether urban or rural. A number of birds, animals and insects feed on them and are maintained by their presence. We need to broaden our vocabulary to differentiate between exotic species and the more problematic subset of these that have become invasive, and to integrate naturalized species within our definitions of the native.

More recently, some scholars have begun challenging conventional wisdom that has created these dichotomies of native and exotic. They say that the animosity towards exotics is a form of indoctrination not supported by strong scientific evidence. They acknowledge the harm that some exotic invasives can cause, but caution that we need to rethink our current bias against all exotics. Cities are novel ecosystems with highly modified landscapes that are in many ways different from the natural ecosystems on which they were built. In such ecologies, isn't there a role for exotic species?

The shade cast by the canopy of the exotic rain tree and the native peepul are appreciated by those bearing the brunt of the scorching temperatures in Indian cities. In fact, many cities across the world are already gearing up to meet the challenge posed by climate change and urban heat island effects. Exotics from Japan and China are being raised in an experimental nursery in Germany and may provide the next generation of trees that line German streets in an attempt to keep the cities cool. Similarly, the exotic African tulip and the naturalized tamarind both support biodiversity in Indian cities. Quite unsurprisingly, this approach has triggered much controversy.

The debate of native versus exotic continues to be controversial, and the scientific debate rages on. What is clear, though, is that the binaries of native and exotic are too simplistic a way to look at trees in cities. We need to decide what trees to plant keeping in mind existing local, social and ecological contexts, and to plan for a future where we may see drastic alterations in climate. Understanding the science behind these terms, looking at people's preferences and bringing in additional distinctions between invasive and naturalized species can help us move beyond this polarized debate.

FOURTEEN

SCARLET
SILK COTTON

The scarlet red silk-cotton tree is most vibrant and at its colourful best in the pre-monsoon season. Devoid of leaves between January and March, the tree may appear dull with its characteristic spiky greyish bark, a sight that is redeemed by the striking large, red flowers that cover the entire canopy. A few weeks later, the large seed pods burst, releasing cotton-like fibre that is used to stuff mattresses, pillows and razais — just in time for the winter. Birds, bees and butterflies feast on the nectar of the tree, which is found across Indian cities but is most widely distributed in north India and characteristic of cities like New Delhi and Jaipur.

The red silk cotton is majestic and a tree of grandeur. In its native habitat, the forests of temperate and tropical Asia, it is a massive emergent tree. In the sandy soil near riverbanks, where it is often found, the tree juts out high into the sky and can be seen for miles around. If you are trekking in the forest without a landmark, having an emergent silk cotton can be a lifesaver, helping you reorient — quite like walking in Paris with the Eiffel Tower helping you find your way, or in Japan next to Mount Fuji.

The tree has an unmistakeable appearance. The bark is an unusual silvery grey when young. The main trunk stands tall and straight, with large branches that jut out horizontally, almost like the ribs of a giant umbrella. This is why the tree is sometimes called the umbrella tree too. But then, this is a tree with many names. Called *semal* in Hindi, it is also the *shalmali* in Sanskrit, *tera* in Manipuri, *buruga* in Kannada and Telugu, and *savar* in Marathi.

The bark of the young tree is covered with large, cone-shaped prickles or thorns. It is an adaptation that the tree developed in its native forest habitat to discourage animals from feeding on it. This is especially useful in cities, where the silk cotton can grow to great heights, undisturbed by goats and cattle. But even these thorns are not enough to keep the tree safe from humans. People cut and grind the thorns into a paste, to make a face pack that treats skin troubles such as acne, and even headaches. When older, the bark turns grey-brown and the prickles often disappear, especially near the base, though you may still see some younger branches covered with thorns.

A full-sized adult tree can grow up to 40 metres, or even taller, although the trees we see in cities are typically smaller. The tree can seem to be almost as thick as it is tall, especially at the base. A giant silk cotton tree in Nandhaur Wildlife Sanctuary, Uttarakhand, is 36 metres tall and 16 metres in circumference. Believed to be between 150 and 200 years old, it takes at least a dozen people to be able to hug it completely. In all likelihood, there are silk cotton trees that are even larger and yet to be measured.

The roots of the red silk-cotton tree need to support a tree of such height. To protect the trunk from falling during monsoon storms, the tree develops buttresses at the base. Just like the stone and cement buttresses built against the wall of many old churches support their height, the buttresses of the silk-cotton tree are large and wide, looking quite like planks or wings that are curved and attached to the base of the tree with glue.

A similar-looking tree, the kapok or *Ceiba pentandra*, is also colloquially called the silk cotton, but it is found in the tropical regions of the Americas and West Africa. In West Africa, the buttresses of the kapok can be of such uniform thickness that many native tribes carve out sections of the buttress and use them as doors to their homes. Columbus, on his first voyage to the West Indies, found native tribes using the hollow trunk of this tree to carve out canoes — one canoe, dug out of a single tree, was large enough to accommodate 150 people. In India, our red silk cotton can be used to make ships and catamarans. But though the tree is large, its wood is soft unlike the wood of the kapok. The red silk-cotton is not very useful as a timber tree and, therefore, cannot be used to make solid, big furniture. The wood is used to make matches, coffins and smaller items like toys and spoons. Some tribal communities, such as the Kathodis of Rajasthan, also use it to make musical instruments such as the dholak and tambura.

The red silk-cotton tree loses all its leaves after the end of the monsoon and presents a very striking appearance between January and April, before the first shower of spring. Naked and leafless, the tree looks like a sculpture of bare branches in January. Soon, the first flowers begin to appear. The blossoms are large, in keeping with the size of the tree. The beautiful red flowers remain tightly closed during the day, opening only in the evening. Throughout the day and well into the night, the flowering tree is covered with insects and birds, some seeking out the nectar, others visiting to drink the water that gathers at the base of the flower, and still others flying in to eat the insect buffet on offer. The birds push their beaks into the flowers to collect the nectar as well as the water that it stores in its cup-shaped bottom end. The flower is craftily designed, so that when the birds pull their beaks out, they are dusted with a coating of pollen. On the next visit, the birds pass on the pollen to the flowers, pollinating them — a win-win situation for both the tree and the bird. Interestingly, the flower is a favourite of the Hanuman langur.

Silk-cotton flowers are widely used, from the preparation of Holi colours to spices. Like the amaltas, a powder from the silk-cotton flower is popular in eco-friendly Holi celebrations — something you can keep in mind for next time. The flowers and young calyx (the part below the flower with the green sepals) are cooked in curries and eaten by many forest tribes, and can be dried and ground into flour, stored for other times of the year. The inner part of the flower is an important spice in Thai cooking. In Maharashtra and Karnataka, the buds are plucked before they mature. They are dried and used as a spice (Marathi *moggu*). Young roots and even young bark can be eaten in times of famine. The flower can also be soaked, ground into a paste and applied on sores and boils — a useful trick to know.

It is not just the flower that has medicinal properties. All parts of the tree — bark, fruit, gum, leaf, seed, root and even the spiny prickles on the trunk — are used to prepare herbal and Ayurvedic medicines. The roots can be roasted and eaten, particularly during times of famine. Also, various parts of the tree can be used to treat an impressive range of diseases, from anaemia to infertility.

But the silk-cotton tree is most famous for the silky threads that are stuffed inside the seed capsule. During colonial times, experiments were made using the cotton, which is very light and water-resistant, to create lifebuoys. The *Indian Textile Journal* reported, tantalizingly, that, 'A man weighing 132 pounds was let down one of the deep wells in the gardens' (with a belt of oil cloth, stuffed with silk cotton, tied around his waist). The belt 'not only kept him suspended in the water with ease, but he was able to carry at the same time in his hands a dead weight of twenty pounds'. These experiments, however successful, do not appear to have taken off, as we do not hear of silk cotton life jackets in use today. The fibres are short and brittle, and cannot be stretched and spun into thread or cloth. They are, however, soft, white and fluffy, and used across India to stuff pillows, mattresses, and even insulating hot-case boxes and soundproof covers.

As children, we used to play with the floating silk-cotton seeds for hours on end during the summer. The lightest breeze is enough to set the seeds floating through the air – the game we played was to blow them from place to place, always making sure that the seed did not land on the ground, or on any surface. Whoever could keep the seed afloat for the longest time won the game. Of course, this could only be played when there was no breeze, which is why the summer vacation months, still and windless, were perfect for this game. In north Indian cities, the silk-cotton tree is often planted in parks. It is common to see families collect under the tree in the summer, with everyone, from grandparents to toddlers, engaged in collecting the seed pods, taking them home and extracting the white fluffy threads that they could either use themselves or sell to mattress makers.

The summer months were also the time when Indians would get their mattresses opened to have them restuffed or fluffed up. Itinerant families in the mattress trade would go along the road, calling out to customers. This process is known in Telugu as *doodhi ekadam* (where 'doodhi' in Telugu means cotton and 'ekadam' refers to separating) and is traditionally conducted by the Dhunia community. The Dhunias carry a stringed instrument with a vibrating bowstring. The strings are plucked, with a loud twang, to announce their arrival in the neighbourhood, and the same instrument is used to clean and fluff the cotton. The sound of the instrument would inform residents that it was time to take out the silk-cotton pods, collected from the trees in the backyard or the neighbourhood and carefully stored over the year. It would be a sight to see—with all the children gathered around to watch, as the stitching on the side of the mattresses and pillows would be carefully unpicked and the silk cotton extracted. After months of use, the cotton filling that would have clumped into hard pockets would be disentangled, fluffed up and evenly stuffed back, sometimes fresh cotton added, after which the mattresses and pillows would be stitched up. The process took an entire day. The courtyard would be covered with wisps of cotton puffs flying all around, getting into ears and noses, making everyone sneeze. It was a joy to sleep on the rejuvenated mattresses again though, at least for a while, until they became misshapen and lumpy again a few months later. With today's mattresses of foam and spring, the use of silk cotton is fading except in small towns in India, where the tree is still prized. But the cotton produced was excellent stuffing for pillows, far more comfortable and environmentally friendly compared to the foam stuffing used today. It is very rare to see Dhunias in cities now. Many of them have in fact shifted to a range of other occupations.

The red silk-cotton is not the only tree from which cotton is produced—far from it. From Alexander's army, which came to India in 326 BC, to Al Beruni, who visited Gujarat in the eleventh century, and British explorers in various parts of India, a number of historical accounts describe the widespread presence of cottons spun from other trees. The Portuguese and British brought in the related sea island cotton from Brazil, which became popular in various parts of India. The cotton from these trees, prized for their fine quality, was used to produce excellent muslins. The cotton fibres they produced were relatively long and could be woven easily, unlike the coarser fibre of the red silk cotton, which could only be used for stuffing. In the eighteenth and nineteenth centuries, India was a surplus producer of these extra-long cottons. But the diversity of cottons that India once produced from various species of tree cottons have now largely disappeared from our collective memory. We no longer have the cultural knowledge about how to use them, or the ecological knowledge of how to maintain and cultivate them.

The red silk-cotton is valued for more than its cotton, the spices from the flowers, and its medicinal properties. The tree plays a major role in traditional myths from different regions of India. In some regions, people believe it to be very inauspicious, even haunted. Other communities protect and worship the tree. It also finds a mention in very old texts. The Mahabharata talks of Bhishma, the *pitamah* (father), taking shelter under a shalmali tree. The ancient sage Yajnavalkya is believed to have called it one of the trees from hell. Because of its forbidding appearance, with thorns embedded in the trunk, it is also called the tree of Yama (the god of death). The Bhil tribes of Udaipur refuse to sleep on silk-cotton mattresses, believing they may be struck with paralysis. Legend has it that Guru Nanak, the founder of Sikhism, did not think much of the tree, considering its looks deceptive and the fruit useless. Bhai Gurudas, the first scribe of the Guru Granth Sahib, also dismissed the tree. While other fruit-laden trees bent down to the flowing river in humility, offering their fruits to help the birds, he said that this tree illustrated ego and lack of altruism, standing tall and proud, bearing only scentless, nauseating flowers, tasteless fruits and useless leaves.

But the tree is culturally valued in other communities. For people born in the Jyeshtha nakshatra (a lunar star sign associated with the zodiac sign of Scorpio), this tree is considered especially sacred. They are believed to benefit from planting this tree. Some tribes in Rajasthan consider it bad luck to cut this tree down, while others believe that the tree harbours *yakshi*s (female earth spirits who get angry if the tree is cut). The tree is worshipped by childless women, who believe that they will be granted the gift of fertility. However, the most widespread impact perhaps comes from the Holika tradition, where branches or young trees of silk cotton are associated with Prahlāda's wicked aunt, Holika, and burnt during Holika Dahan festivities in north India. One study in Udaipur district, in 2007, found close to 2500 trees and branches burnt in a single day. Thus, the sacred traditions associated with the silk-cotton tree can both protect and harm the tree.

The silk cotton is a good tree to plant in cities for many other reasons. It can be planted in degraded soil and flourishes even in very dry conditions, with little water — all it demands is sufficient sunlight as it does not grow well in the shade. It rarely grows on its own in cities, but with planting and a little care it can thrive for decades. Silk-cotton trees in the grounds around the Taj Mahal in Agra and near the Gateway of India in Mumbai offer visitors respite from the baking sun, while decades-old silk-cotton trees provide many parts of Delhi, like the diplomatic avenues of Neeti Marg and the lawns of Teen Murti Bhavan, their characteristic identity.

A number of cities across the world prize the silk-cotton tree. Both the Taiwanese port city of Kaohsiung and the Chinese riverine city of Guangzhou have selected the showy silk-cotton blossom as their city flower. In north-west Vietnam, a number of tourist destinations showcase their centuries-old silk-cotton trees, whose scarlet blossoms dominate the landscape. Local residents believe that the blossoms are a sign that it is time to put away warm blankets – the end of winter. This species is particularly useful in cities given its capacity to reduce overall air pollution and sulphur dioxide content. Despite what Guru Nanak may have thought, the flowers contain a lot of nectar and attract a variety of birds, butterflies, bees and other insects. Thus the silk-cotton acts as a keystone species in cities, supporting many other forms of biodiversity, including langurs and squirrels. Bats and bees nest on the tree and its sharp thorns protect it from stray cows, helping young saplings to flourish.

The silk-cotton fibres form an important component of urban livelihoods, especially for communities in small towns, who continue to be traditionally involved in making mattresses and pillows. Fallen leaves and flowers are also rich in protein, valuable for urban gardeners who want to make vermicompost. It is culturally important to different communities in varied ways – worshipped by some, feared by others. But anyone who has seen the spectacular sight of the large scarlet blossoms of the tree, silhouetted against its spiky, leafless silvery grey branches, cannot fail to have been mesmerized.

Red silk cotton (*Bombax ceiba*)

Description: Large and lofty tree that can grow quite tall. Lower part of the trunk is covered with conical prickles and with a buttressed base. Bark is silvery-grey.

Flowers: Scarlet, showy flowers, with thick, waxy petals. They stand out as the tree is leafless during blooming season.

Fruits: Woody capsule that splits open to reveal silky strands of cotton amidst which small seeds are embedded.

Leaves: Smooth lance-shaped leaflets.

Seasonality: Deciduous tree whose leaves start falling in December and extending into March. Flowering is between January and March while fruiting starts in March and extends into May, with fruit pods ripening and splitting.

Family: Bombacaceae. Members of this family have showy flowers, but also serve commercial and economic purposes.

Origin and distribution: Native to India and widely distributed across the country, except in very arid parts.

FIFTEEN

THE
FELLOWSHIP
OF **THE GROVE**

Since ancient times, cities have been founded after destroying forests and trees, as told to us in myths, legends and historical narratives. The Khandava forest in the Mahabharata was burnt down by Arjuna and Krishna to establish the city of Indraprastha (believed to be modern-day New Delhi). The medieval town of Bengaluru was built by clearing out a jungle. Alongside this destruction of forests, new urban settlers planted and nurtured trees in and around cities. Groves of fruit-bearing trees seemed to have covered the landscape in different parts of the country, used as sites for the collection of fruit, as well as for community gathering.

Ashoka, the Mauryan emperor, planted mango orchards with wells throughout his kingdom to ensure shade and water for travellers in the third century BC. Mughal rulers Babur, who ruled in the sixteenth century CE, and Dara Shikoh, who came in the seventeenth century CE, were both mango lovers. Their memoirs describe orchards of some of the finest mango trees planted around towns and cities. So favoured was this fruit that Mughal noblemen who raised mango orchards were granted tax waivers. This tradition of planting fruit groves continued into colonial times as well. A number of British gazetteers from the early 1900s mention groves across north India. In Agra, 4 per cent of the land area was covered by groves of mango, jamun, bael and other indigenous fruit. In Jhansi, the tamarind was a favourite tree of the ruling Maratha kings. It was planted widely, encouraged by rent-free grants of land. Lucknow had groves of mango and orchards of ber, covering 22,059 acres in the district in 1866, while Kanpur had several thousand acres covered by mango and mahua. The main civil station of Ganjam (present-day Srikakulam in Andhra Pradesh) was 'well studded with mango and tamarind topes' (topes means orchards), while the town of Ellore (today's Eluru) had extensive groves of toddy. Across the Deccan and the southern peninsula, groves of mango, neem, banyan and tamarind were in abundance.

Groves gave their name to many towns. The town of Hazaribagh (the garden of a thousand trees) in Bihar, got its name from a massive mango grove with thousands of trees. The grove was so large that it is said to have provided a camping ground for troops travelling between Kolkata and Varanasi. Similarly, the city of Ambala near Chandigarh derives its name from Ambwala (land of mangoes), in tribute to its numerous mango groves. The names of localities in many cities also give us an indication of the groves that once stood there. In Chennai, we have Pelathope (jackfruit orchard), Mambalam (mango fruit), Vepery (neem), Teynampet (coconut), Panayur (palm village), Alandur (banyan), and Illuppaithoppu (mahua orchard), for instance. In Bengaluru, we have Halasur (jackfruit orchard) and Gundathope (*gunda thope* being the local name for a wooded grove). Mumbai too was covered with groves of different species. Phanaswadi derives its name from a jackfruit orchard that once flourished there, Vadala from a banyan grove and Madmala or Manmala (today's crowded Mahim), from the orchard of coconuts. Do we even know how many localities in the towns and cities we live in today are named after such groves?

Groves were built and maintained by local residents, who received tax relief. William Sleeman, a British officer, in his memoir *Rambles and Recollections of an Indian Official*, wrote about groves in Jabalpore (now Jabalpur) in 1828. He said that land was provided rent-free to locals on the condition that the person would plant and care for twenty-five trees per acre. They were meant for more than providing fruit, however. The owner was also expected to build and maintain a well to water the trees, and to provide drinking water to travellers. The same officer describes a fascinating story of a Hindu couple, Berjore Sing and his wife (sadly unnamed), who owned a mango grove. According to local custom, they could not taste the fruit from the grove unless they married one of the trees, or the grove itself, to a nearby tree (normally a tamarind). The poor couple spent so much on planting and maintaining their grove and wells that they could not conduct the wedding for years, since they never had enough money. But fearing that they would die without tasting the mangoes from their orchard, which their children had eaten and spoke highly of, Sing and his wife sold their gold and silver ornaments, even borrowing money to hold the marriage. Around 150 Brahmin guests were invited to the feast. In the meantime, the only tamarind in their grove had died. Sing married the tree to a jasmine vine he had planted next to the mango tree that had been chosen as the bridegroom for the occasion. In the next fruiting season, in June 1834, Sing and his wife tasted the fruit from their trees, satisfied at last, happy that they were able to do so before they left this world. This touching story gives us a glimpse into how deeply these groves were interwoven into the lives of their owners, being much more than mere sources of income.

One of India's earliest naturalists E.H. Aitken, writing about mango groves, asks, 'Where would the dusty wayfarer stop to eat his midday chuppattee [flat bread made of wheat flour] and drink a draught of cold water, or where would the collector pitch his tent?'

In Mysuru, Hyder Ali is believed to have encouraged the development of gunda thopes across the region. This practice was continued by the Mysore government during the colonial period. The *Mysore Gazetteer* counts 2118 gunda thopes in 1894, spread across Bengaluru (then Bangalore) district, containing mango, jamun, mahua, jackfruit, tamarind and different species of ficus. Travelling along the periphery of the city, the remnants of these groves can be seen even today. Wood from trees in the groves (preferably from mango trees) was used for construction or renovation of temples, and for building doors and windows of homes. The poor, who had no land or trees of their own, were permitted to cut branches to use during weddings and cremations. Community meetings and festival feasts were held under the shade of the trees. Fruits of the mango and tamarind were shared among the families and auctioned to fund village development. Cows, goats and sheep were brought to the thopes to escape the heat of the midday sun, after being washed and given water in lakes nearby. While the grazers dozed or meditatively stared into space, the animals nibbled on the undergrowth protected by the shade of the trees.

The thopes also offered temporary residence to nomadic communities, wandering mendicants and astrologers. The trees themselves were once believed to be the abode of gods and climbing them was forbidden. Some thopes had small shrines and stones at the base of trees, dedicated to local deities. In some of the remnant groves, grazing still persists and time seems to stand still, except when the honk of a passing vehicle brings us back to the present. But even today at dusk, the sound of vehicles is drowned by the cacophony of birds that come to the thopes to roost for the night, amidst the fruit bats that can be seen flitting around the trees.

Groves around towns in north India, situated along the banks of the Ganga, had other uses. They provided cover for Indian sepoys and British troops during the famous 1857 revolts against colonial rule. We can get a glimpse of the beauty of these groves that seem to have dotted the landscape from the memoirs of James Forbes who came to India as a writer for the East India Company and spent nearly two decades here. Forbes travelled extensively, especially in northern India, and mentioned the many groves he saw in *Oriental Memoirs,* published in 1834. Describing the province of Gujarat, he said that 'the number of trees which adorn the roads, the richness of the mango topes around the villages, the size and verdure of the tamarind trees, clothe the country with uncommon beauty, such indeed as I never saw to so great an extent in any other part of the globe'.

Where are these urban groves and orchards that once covered hundreds of acres? They have been lost over the years as cities grew. We can still find some remnants in some cities, but these are increasingly in danger of being lost, cut down to make way for roads and buildings. Few of Bengaluru's groves exist today. Many have been degraded, with hardly any trees, while others have been turned into dumping sites, or converted to schools, roads, bus stops, community centres or houses. Some have been converted into parks, landscaped and beautified so much so that the original grove is unrecognizable. The trails where once cattle trod have been replaced by paved paths. What is saddest is the fading of the groves from the collective memory of the community. A once-vibrant urban ecosystem central to daily living is being reduced to an overgrown patch of land devoid of trees. As the city expands, more and more of these gunda thopes will be lost. But can knowing about the existence of these groves, and similar patches in other cities be the first step towards protecting them?

Another wilderness, located at the edge of the capital city of New Delhi, holds out hope, continuing to hang on (by a narrow thread of safety) amidst the increasing pressures of urbanization. Mangarbani is a sacred grove situated close to Gurugram, the satellite city of New Delhi, in the state of Haryana. A relatively undisturbed forest, Mangarbani has a shrine dedicated to Gudariya Baba, a hermit revered by the local villages. According to the communities living around this grove, grazing livestock and cutting wood in the grove could incur the wrath of the baba, resulting in the death of livestock or wooden beams in houses catching fire. This belief has ensured that the grove stayed protected over the years.

The land around the grove was categorized as *shamilat-deh* (local commons), on which the landless poor depend for wood for cooking and fodder for animals. The relentless growth of real estate around the National Capital Region (NCR) now threatens the future of this heritage grove. Many local residents have come together to protect the grove, supported by activist groups from Delhi.

Mangarbani forms a part of the Aravalli range. Its trees show us what these ancient hills once looked like. Unlike the Delhi Ridge, whose forests have been overrun by the exotic invasive mesquite, Mangarbani continues to be covered with native species. Even today, the grove is a valley of green with many species of native trees bursting into colour with the blossoming of the red palash and the striking yellow amaltas in the spring.

Meanwhile, other cities across the world have found a way to coexist with their groves. Just thirty minutes from the frenzied chaos of Kyoto is the Sagano bamboo forest, a spectacular natural grove that regularly makes it to travellers' bucket lists. It is a tourist attraction that draws visitors from across the world. A few kilometres from Ghana's capital city, Accra, is the Guako sacred grove, where the blacksmith god Nii Gua is worshipped. Accra is the most densely populated of Ghana's cities. Despite the pressure of urban growth, the Greater Accra development plan identifies and aims to protect the sacred grove, and environmental organizations such as Friends of Earth run programmes aimed at educating the public about its significance.

The term 'urbanization' conjures up images of the relentless expansion of cities, progressively sprawling into the surroundings. What is lost in this process, and then quickly forgotten, are the majestic gunda thopes of Bengaluru and heritage groves such as Mangarbani. Gone with the trees is the ethic that motivated these groves. Planting trees was considered a charitable act, something that conferred religious merit. Caring for these groves was a collective responsibility. Mangarbani is not just a piece of real estate but a sacred grove that is also a refuge for all forms of biodiversity. Gunda thopes once met the livelihood, social and cultural needs of local communities.

How many similar wooded groves existed across cities in India? We will probably never know. A narrative from Lucknow makes us pause. The name *sakhya* (derived from the word *saakhi* or witness), says the district gazetteer of 1904, was used to refer to solitary mango trees, the only witnesses to locations where flourishing groves once stood, a fellowship of trees maintained by the collective action of local communities. What a loss it would be, not just to our ecologies but also our social lives, if all that was left to remind us of these wooded groves once flourishing around our cities were such solitary witnesses.

SIXTEEN

NEEM:
THE BITTER
TREE OF WELLNESS

It is hard to imagine life in India without the neem. Our grandparents brushed their teeth with neem twigs — many of them retained their teeth and lived until their nineties. We place dried neem leaves under the newspaper lining in our cupboards to protect woollens from an insect attack. Also, we use neem paste as part of home remedies — from face packs for teenage acne to tea for senior citizens suffering from diabetes, and gargles for sore throats.

The neem has been around for a long time. Harappan pottery from Mohenjo-daro depicts the neem tree, with a stick-like figure sitting on its branches. One hand is stretched towards a tiger that looks at the figure over its shoulder. Sometimes, the tiger wears a pair of zebu (Indian cattle) horns. Some historians think the tree may have been a part of Harappan shamanic rituals. Neem also had more prosaic uses. Wood charcoal remains from various Harappan settlements show us that the inhabitants burnt neem wood. Pottery jars with neem and other medicinal leaves suggest that they were used to prepare medicines.

CITIES AND CANOPIES · 154

The famous *Arthashastra*, from the second–third centuries CE, tells us about commercial neem oil extraction. In some detail, the book tells you that the amount of oil you can extract from neem seeds will be one-fifth of the quantity of the seeds you provide. The popular name, neem or nim is derived from the Sanskrit word *nimba* (to bestow health). It has several other names too given its usefulness — village pharmacy, healing tree, divine tree, nature's drugstore and *kalpavriksh* of Kalyuga (the wish-fulfilling tree in the age of Kali). Many Sanskrit medical texts refer to it as *sarva roga nivarini* (the tree that cures all illnesses). The scientific name of neem, *Azadirachta indica*, however comes from another source. It is derived from the Farsi word *azadarakhat*. While the exact meaning is contested, most people say the name is derived from *Azad-darakhat-e Hind* (free tree of India). There are some though who say the name comes from *aza darakhat* (bitter tree).

The flowers are not as bitter, giving out a very delicate fragrance that perfumes the area in which the tree is planted, attracting a number of bees, butterflies and even bats. In Andhra Pradesh, Telangana, Tamil Nadu and Kerala, you cannot celebrate the new year without neem flowers. The flowers are carefully separated from the stems and used to make the ugadi (new year) pachadi (chutney). The dish combines a variety of flavours — sweet, sour, salty, bitter and spicy (using chilly). The different flavours symbolize what life might have to offer in the year ahead and remind us to make the best of the different flavours the year holds. We can understand just how important the neem flower is from the experience of the coastal city of Visakhapatnam, after Cyclone Hudhud in 2014. The cyclone destroyed many trees across the city. The next year's ugadi pachadi was affected because of the scarcity of neem flowers, which once grew abundantly in the city and could be bought cheaply from the local vegetable vendor. This news made its way to headlines in the local newspapers: 'Hudhud has its impact on ugadi pachadi'.

Other cuisines also value the neem. In Bengal, at the start of spring, when the new reddish-brown, tender leaves of the neem emerge, they are plucked and used to make neem bhaja (roast vegetable). Eggplants are roasted in oil, tender neem leaves are fried to a crisp and added to this signature Bengali dish. It is one of those dishes you either hate or love. It is eaten because it cleanses your stomach, protects you from colds when the weather changes and stimulates your appetite.

The magic properties of this amazing tree are not just valued at home but also commercially. It has, in fact, led to heated international patent battles. In 1995, the European Patent Office granted a patent to the United States Department of Agriculture and a large American company that had developed an extract of neem oil, which they called Neemix, to combat fungal growth. Scathing criticisms poured in from India and outside. Many saw this as a new kind of colonialism where knowledge from developing countries, such as India, was stolen by the West. Others said that patenting neem was morally wrong as it was a plant considered sacred in India. Such companies made millions of dollars from patents that were never shared with the countries or communities from where the tree was originally taken.

Farmers in India have used neem oil for centuries for precisely the same purpose, but they lacked a paper trail, such as publications in peer-reviewed journals, that could prove this use. Despite centuries of traditional knowledge about the neem, India was in danger of losing intellectual property rights to its use. A global coalition—Free the Free Tree—came together for this purpose. It included Indian environmentalists and scientists, as well as international groups, who battled the patent for ten years.

In neighbouring Bangladesh, where farmers also use the neem, a massive demonstration was held against the patent. Close to half a million people attended this protest. The coalition finally won the case in 2005 and the neem patent was cancelled. Though other US patents on neem are still around, this victory helped establish a precedent that traditional knowledge belongs to the place and people who have used it for centuries.

The neem is found across Indian cities. Begur, one of the older settlements of Bengaluru, is said to derive its name from Veppuru (*vepa* being neem tree in Tamil and Telugu). Margosa Road in Bengaluru is named after the neem trees that were planted there. In Hyderabad, a neem tree in Sri Ujjaini Mahakali temple is dated back to 1813. Suriti Appaiah, a doli-bearer (who carried stretchers in the medical unit of the army) from Hyderabad was posted in the city of Ujjain. On hearing of the cholera epidemic in Hyderabad, Appaiah and his associates prayed at the Mahakali temple in Ujjain, promising to install an idol of the goddess in Hyderabad if the epidemic was controlled. When he returned to Hyderabad in 1815, Appaiah kept his promise installing a wooden idol of Mahakali and is said to have also planted the neem tree.

The tree still stands in the temple today. No one is allowed to pluck the leaves, only the priests use them during festivals. During the annual Bonalu festivities, women carry pots filled with rice, turmeric, jaggery and curd, decorated with neem leaves, as an offering to Mahakali to seek protection in warding off diseases. Neem is believed to be the abode of Shitala, the goddess of smallpox, to whom offerings are made to keep away chickenpox, smallpox and other skin diseases. When children get chickenpox, they are bathed in water in which neem leaves are immersed. The rashes on their skin are soothed with neem leaves. In south India, especially in Tamil Nadu, the goddess of smallpox is called Mariamman.

Neem flowers and leaves are an essential part of the Mariamman temple festivals each year in villages and towns across south India. The neem is also often 'married' to the peepul tree in a symbolic ceremony for fertility and auspiciousness.

The British found it to be a tree both beautiful and useful. A British visitor to India, Anne Katherine Elwood, wrote in the 1820s, 'The neem is most peculiarly light and elegant in its appearance, somewhat resembling a young acacia or mountain ash, whilst its cluster of flowers are not dissimilar to those of the lilac, and are delightfully fragrant.' The British planted it widely across India in the 1880s. But as the British foresters were known to do, they were obsessed with figuring out the best way to germinate the seeds.

Some foresters seemed to have difficulty germinating neem seeds, while others found that the neem seeds collected from bird droppings germinated well. To test this, foresters from the Forest Resource Institute in Dehradun tried out a hilarious experiment with chickens in 1938, trying to get them to eat neem fruits. Not surprisingly, the chickens 'turned up their beaks in scorn'. The poor birds were then put on a starvation diet and again offered the fruit. Despite being desperately hungry, they refused the fruits, but finally ate them when they were disguised in flour. The forester then waited for days, feeding the birds hearty meals and closely inspecting the droppings. But days after the seeds were consumed, they could see no sign of them in the droppings. The unobliging birds were finally returned to their owners, which must have relieved the chickens tremendously.

Bizarre germination experiments aside, the neem is favoured for planting in cities for a variety of reasons. Neem is an easy species to raise and a hardy tree that can survive nibbling by goats and cattle—a constant hazard in Indian cities. It is also popular because of the belief that the tree provides healthy air and purifies water. The tree is resistant to pollution as well. Sabarmati Ashram in Ahmedabad, Mahatma Gandhi's abode for many years, was planted with neem trees by a resident, Totaram. Neem was a favourite of Gandhi's and he ate neem chutney regularly. On Gandhi's suggestion, Totaram collected neem seedlings from villages around, planted them with care and gave them water from the Sabarmati, on whose banks the ashram was situated. Neem trees stand tall in the ashram even today.

Neem has also made it to the deserts of Africa and the Middle East. In Sudan, as far back as 1939, an account in the *Indian Forester* talks of widespread planting of the neem, which was used for firewood and for timber to build houses. The largest neem plantation with 50,000 trees over 10 sq. km was undertaken in the Plain of Arafat in Saudi Arabia, to provide shade to the millions who camp here during the Haj pilgrimage. This was one of the rare trees that could withstand the harsh and dry climate, even temperatures up to 50° C. It is fascinating that a tree from India was chosen to provide shade to Haj pilgrims. In northern Australia, though, it has become an invasive species, spreading into waterways and choking them. It has now been declared a noxious weed in some areas and the Australian government puts in much effort into controlling its spread. It is strange that what is so prized in one location is deeply disliked and damaging in another.

The neem continues to be a tree of everyday use in India. There is now a growing movement in some cities to return to the eco-friendly *datun* (neem toothbrush), which can be used and disposed of, and is plastic-free compared to the toothbrushes of today. There is also a village called Danton on the border of West Bengal and Odisha. The story goes that Chaitanya Mahaprabhu, the Hindu mystic and saint, while on a pilgrimage to the temple town of Puri in Odisha, halted for the night at this village. The next morning, he used the twigs of the neem to clean his teeth, giving the village the name Danton.

The tree is a pharmacy in itself. Fermented toddy can be made using neem as well, in addition to the more common palm. Gum or resin can be tapped from the tree by making a wound in the bark. Some older trees, meanwhile, exude the gum naturally. When this happens, a phenomenon referred to as weeping, the gum is much prized, collected and stored as a tonic. Neem oil can also be sprayed as a natural pesticide in gardens. Strangely though, the tree is not always able to protect itself from a fungal or insect attack. In Bengaluru, a fungal disease known as dieback of neem is causing these trees to dry up. In Hyderabad, neem trees are being attacked by a parasite, Loranthus (honeysuckle mistletoe), and by the scale insect *Aonidiella orientalis*. So, if you notice any blighting of twigs and flowers, or rotting of fruit, the neem may need you to turn pharmacist and help it out.

Alan Butterworth in *Some Madras Trees*, published in 1911, says about the neem that it is, 'One of the commonest tree of the country, so common that I hesitate to describe it were it not that a friend of mine reached the rank of Acting Collector without knowing the tree.' This should continue to be unacceptable. We should all know about the neem, its many benefits and perhaps spend more time under its canopy to get to know it better.

Neem (*Azadirachta indica*)

Description: Medium-sized tree with a shady canopy. Trunk is short with a fissured bark that is dark grey on the outside.

Flowers: Tiny and fragrant with creamish-white petals.

Fruits: Egg-shaped fruit about 1–2 cm long, with a little pulp around a hard seed. Green initially but turns yellow when ripe.

Leaves: Feather-like, slightly curved with serrated edges.

Seasonality: Evergreen, though the tree does shed some leaves in the dry season. Flowers can start appearing in February, extending to May. Fruits ripen between June and August.

Family: Meliaceae. Family has several species whose timber is of high value, such as mahogany trees.

Origin and distribution: Origins not entirely clear, but it is found across India, except in places with frost.

Recipe for Ugadi Gojju or Pachadi

Carefully extract neem flowers from the stalk, making sure there are no stems. (One way to do this is to pick them off one by one. Another easier way, if you are cooking in bulk, is to place the entire stem with flowers on to a damp white towel. The flowers will stick to the towel and can be later shaken off.) Take a deep-bottomed kadai (thick saucepan) and heat a couple of tablespoons of ghee. Add the neem flowers and roast at medium heat until the flowers turn reddish. Add half a cup of watery tamarind pulp, a slit green chilli and cook for ten minutes. Add salt (to taste), a pinch or spoon of red chilli powder (depending on how spicy you want it) and a small walnut-sized lump of jaggery. Cook till the jaggery dissolves. In a separate vessel, add ghee and some mustard seeds for seasoning. Once the mustard seeds splutter, add fenugreek seeds, asafoetida, curry leaves and a dried red chilli or two, roasting the mix for a couple of minutes on low flame. Turn off the flame and add the seasoning to the pachadi.

SEVENTEEN

AN INORDINATE
FONDNESS
FOR TREES

British ecologist J.B.S. Haldane, a giant in the field of evolutionary biology, is credited with saying that God must have an inordinate fondness for beetles, since there were so many kinds of beetles in the world. We can safely presume, perhaps, that God also has an inordinate fondness for trees — given the number and kinds there are in the world.

There are tall trees and short ones, fat-trunked giants and skinny-stemmed upstarts, species that grow furiously but die fast and those that grow slowly but live for thousands of years. Some trees have massive leaves that you can use to dine on, while others have thousands of tiny leaves, or even spiky, needle-like protrusions that look nothing like leaves at all. Some like the silk-cotton tree have majestic buttress roots, which make great living drums for forest tribes to thump on, signalling to others in the distant forest. Others like the neem have narrow tap roots that burrow deep into the ground, leaving no visible sign on the surface; stilt roots like mangrove trees, holding the tree above the surface of salt water; or aerial prop roots like the banyan, growing down from the branches into the soil and helping it to spread across acres. Some trees emit latex that is deadly, while the gum of others is pleasant to taste and can be used in cooking or as medicine.

What stimulates this incredible variety in trees?

The shape, size, type of leaf, time of flowering, leafing and fruiting, type of trunk, bark and root, number of seeds, nature of pollination and dispersal, colour of the flower—all are called traits of the plant or tree. They serve different purposes. The total number and variety of traits are far too much to capture in one chapter, let alone in a single book. A global plant trait database called TRY, hosted by Max Planck Institute for Biogeochemistry and Future Earth, contains information on 6.9 million traits for 148,000 plant species for instance. But it is still interesting to learn about a few of these traits, which can help us understand why some of our favourite trees look and behave the way they do.

Seed size and shape determines the type of dispersal, how far a plant can move away from its parent and how long it can survive without the right kind of soil, sun or water. Seeds that are small and light, like those of the silk-cotton tree, can be easily blown away in the wind and move far away from the parent plant. But if they land in the wrong place, they do not have enough food stored to survive long periods of stress. Seeds like that of the coconut are large and well-protected by a husk. The coconut usually grows in coastal areas, and the nuts fall into the sea water. The thick husk and hard shell help the seed survive for long periods in the harsh salt water, and protect it from being eaten by birds and fish. The water and flesh inside the coconut is rich in nutrients and helps nourish the seed while it germinates.

Leaves come in different shapes and sizes. Larger leaves catch more sunlight, which helps them produce more food. Trees with large leaves survive well in shaded areas, where they need to catch as much sunlight as they can. But if it's too hot and dry, then it's better to have small leaves, as larger leaves also have more surface area and thus lose more water. In cold areas, like in the mountains, where the air is very dry and windy, it is important to conserve water. Pines and other trees with needle-like or spiky leaves grow here. These needles are protected by waxy surfaces that help them retain water. The leaves themselves are thin and the surface is slippery, so that in times of heavy snow, the snow slides down without tearing off the leaves. Imagine a tree with leaves as tender as that of a banana plant in the cold mountains. Sounds like a bad idea!

The time when a tree sheds leaves and grows new ones is also an adaptation to the kind of environment in which a tree evolves. Deciduous trees are largely found in areas where there is a marked difference between seasons, with separate dry and wet seasons, or hot and cold seasons. During the cold or dry season, the trees shed leaves to conserve water. When the time is right, new leaves grow back. Interestingly, some trees like the neem and amla shed their leaves and act like deciduous trees during the hot summers in Delhi, but keep their leaves all year round, like evergreen trees, when they are in moist forests and in areas next to rivers. Pradip Krishen, in his book *Trees of Delhi*, points out that this duplicity confused the British, who planted these trees in the city thinking that they were evergreen, not realizing that there would be a brief time of the year when they would shed most of their leaves.

Avoiding being eaten by insects or animals is another important aspect on which many trees expend a great deal of effort and energy. Some trees like the silk cotton grow spiky thorns on their barks, particularly when they are young and more likely to be eaten by deer, cows and other browsers. Some trees ooze out a poisonous sticky sap from their leaves and bark when damaged. Others, like the eucalyptus, have leaves that taste nasty and can even be poisonous for insects and animals in their new homes in India. But insects co-evolve with trees and plants. In San Joaquim Valley in the USA, eucalyptus trees imported from Australia in the 1850s thrived for 150 years in an environment without pests that could attack them—until the red gum lerp psyllid, its native pest, managed to hitch-hike its way from Australia to California in 1998. The attack of the psyllids was devastating for the eucalyptus trees, until a tiny parasitic wasp (*Psyllaephagus bliteus*), which attacks the psyllid, was identified and brought over from Australia. The wasp ate the psyllid and the psyllid stopped attacking the tree—a long and complicated way to deal with problems caused by importing a species from one location to another.

Flowers use their colour, scent and shape to manipulate birds, insects and other feeders to spread their pollen and seeds around. Insect-pollinated trees have big, showy, colourful flowers with attractive scents that call in the insects from miles away. Bird-pollinated flowers rely on their looks. They are usually either mildly scented or without any scent. But wind-pollinated trees do not need to waste valuable energy on producing large, showy flowers. Their flowers are often small and delicate, though just as beautiful. Of course, to mix things up a bit, some trees are both wind- and insect-pollinated. Trees and plants with small-sized fruits have more flexibility in choice of the time of flowering and fruiting. But trees that bear large fruits need time for the fruits to grow, mature and produce seeds. They need to flower early and fruit early in the spring, so that before the cold weather sets in they can be ready with the seeds.

In cities, many (if not most) trees have been deliberately selected by people, often brought in and planted from distant parts of the world with quite different habitats. Many trees in Indian cities come from very different environments. In some cases this is a good thing for the tree – like the eucalyptus, which came to India but left its pests behind and is thus able to ward off local pests that find its leaves unpalatable. But species like the gulmohar, well adapted to the porous sandy or loamy soils of Madagascar, do not do so well in Indian cities. It is widely planted across many Indian cities for obvious reasons – it is a beautiful tree with an arresting canopy profile and captivating scarlet blossoms that light up the horizon. But its buttress roots do not penetrate deep into the ground, especially in the hardened city roadside soil where it is often planted. In times of rain and wind, the gulmohar is very vulnerable and falls easily, damaging homes and often posing a danger to lives as well.

Other traits do not affect the ecological survival of the tree, but they do impact its selection by the people who plant it. In Delhi, as Pradip Kishen describes, British planners moved away from traditional Indian favourites like the banyan and mango because their canopies were too large and seemed (to them) to be visually overwhelming. Instead, they chose trees like the neem, jamun and tamarind with canopies that were large, but not *too* large. In Bengaluru, German and British horticulturalists selected trees from across the world with overlapping flowering seasons, so that at all times of the year, some flowers would definitely be in bloom, keeping the city well adorned.

We are largely oblivious to the traits of trees today. But these are incredibly important, detailed adaptations, perfected by each species over time periods ranging from thousands to millions of years. Keeping tabs on the traits of the trees you love can be fun, involving observations of fruiting, flowering and pollination, and patient dissections of everything from flowers to fruits and leaves to bark. As long as you don't dig up the roots, or irretrievably damage the tree, it's all fine!

EIGHTEEN

PEEPUL:
THE PEOPLE'S
TREE

It is difficult to imagine Indian cities without the peepul. We tend to associate the tree with temples. But, in reality, one of the most common places where the peepul can be seen is along the roadsides. Sometimes, you can even find a peepul right in the middle of a road, a bright green spot in the midst of swirling traffic. We fail to notice these trees as we carry on with our daily tasks. But look out across your cities, from Kolkata to Mumbai to Delhi, and keep your eyes on the buildings, especially in the older parts. You will see peepul trees, small and large, growing from the crevices of walls and roofs of many old homes. Birds eat the fruits of the peepul and drop the seeds as they fly overhead. Some of these seeds find their way into crevices of walls and roofs, from which we can see the strange sight of brown roots curling around concrete, and shiny green leaves emerging as the young saplings grow. Some trees even grow large, embedding their roots into the wall.

The peepul is one of the easiest trees to recognize. Its leaves are distinctive, shiny, heart-shaped, with wavy edges and a pointed tip. The leaves seem to be in constant motion, fluttering on their long stalks at the slightest sign of a breeze. The sound is like the pattering of raindrops, as the wavy leaves brush against each other. The same tree in the dry season, stripped bare of all its leaves, looks equally majestic. The pale grey bark is framed by branches that reach out towards the sky as it rests, waiting to acquire a fresh set of leaves. The fruit (figs) of the peepul, reddish-purple when they ripen, are a favourite with the birds.

A little known aspect is the ruthless nature of this tree. Like its close cousin, the banyan, the peepul also acts as a strangler fig. Peepul seeds, dropped on to another tree, can grow over the host tree, using it for anchorage and support. As the tree grows, it eventually surrounds and strangles the host. Unlike a parasite, the peepul is what is called an epiphyte — it does not draw sap from the host plant, but makes its own food, taking in nourishment from the sun, air and rain.

The peepul is one of the oldest trees to be recorded in India, depicted in seals and pottery of the Indus Valley civilization. The Rig Veda (from around 3700 BC) talks about the sacred nature of the peepul. Surapala, in the *Vrikshayurveda*, says that, 'He who plants even a single *asvattha* (peepul), wherever it may be, as per the prescribed mode, goes to the abode of Hari.'

In many villages and cities, we find peepul trees on elevated platforms (in Karnataka, these are very popular and are called ashwathkattes). On these platforms, peepul and neem are married to each other in rituals (the peepul is believed to be the male and the neem the female). Snake stones anointed with haldi and kumkum are found on the platform. These kattes are cared for by locals and prayers are offered at these shrines. The peepul is sacred to Hindus as a symbol of fertility. The peepul tree in Bodh Gaya, under which Gautama Buddha attained enlightenment, is an important pilgrimage location for Buddhists.

In addition to the sacred, mundane daily activities also take place under the peepul tree. Flower and fruit sellers sit under the shade in search of shelter, and a range of other items from clothes to helmets are sold under the tree. It is considered dangerous to lie or cheat while sitting under the peepul tree. Thus, many people prefer to plant the peepul in market spaces, both for the shade it provides and to keep traders from cheating. Kattes are also locations where people gather to play a game of cards or chess, chat about local gossip and national politics, or take a nap under the tree's welcoming shade on a hot afternoon.

Peepul leaves are used to feed goats and cows and, in the past, were also used to feed captive elephants. This use is now being re-popularized. In Odisha, peepul trees have been planted in forest fringes to feed wild elephants and prevent them from moving towards towns and cities in search of food. The Santhal and Gond tribes eat the fruit and young leaves as part of their regular diet. Other communities reserve the small figs and the leaf buds as famine food, which supports them in desperate times such as droughts. The bark, leaves, figs and roots have medicinal value. They are used to treat a host of illnesses, including skin disorders, diabetes, and digestive problems. The bark of the peepul is also used to make ropes. These multiple uses — as a source of food, fodder, fibre and medicine — are still known to many rural residents, but have been forgotten by most of us in the cities.

Peepul trees can grow to venerable ages. They are massive trees when fully grown. The peepul is a symbol of India, planted to commemorate special events. In 2015, when former US president Barack Obama visited New Delhi, he planted a peepul tree at Rajghat, the memorial dedicated to Mahatma Gandhi. Older trees have shaped the identity of many cities big and small. A peepul tree inside the Red Fort in the capital city commemorates poignant events in the country's quest for freedom, as many rebels were said to have been hung at this spot by British rulers. In the small west Godavari town of Eluru, a century-old peepul was called the *perugu chettu* (tree of curds). The tree was the centre of a local market for curds and milk. The original tree was uprooted in a cyclone about twenty years ago. A young sapling grew out of its roots, and is now quite tall itself. The curd vendors have moved away, except for a few. But the spot where the tree once stood is still called perugu chettu.

The famous Clock Tower of Dehradun has a heritage peepul that is considered significant in the city. It was planted by Sarojini Naidu. In 2015, the future of the tree was threatened by a proposal to beautify the Clock Tower and a road-widening project. A group of local citizens — Citizens for Green Doon — staged massive protests. They were inspired by the Raksha Sutra Andolan, a movement that started in the Garhwal Hills in 1994, where people tied rakhis to trees, pledging to protect trees. The Citizens for Green Doon wore festive clothes, prayed and also tied rakhis around the peepul's trunk. They were able to save the peepul, which still stands today, a testimony to the heritage of the city and to its citizens who fought to save it.

Ecologically, the peepul is an excellent tree for cities. It acts as a carbon sink and plays a major role in reducing air and noise pollution. The peepul is also a keystone species, supporting a wide range of biodiversity. In a hostile city, where food and shelter are limited, figs of the peepul feed a variety of birds, who also build their nests here. Monkeys relish the fruit, while the slender loris also seeks shelter in the tree. Fruit bats too seek out the tree for roosting. They are a common sight, in the dozens and hundreds, hanging upside down on the peepul, their high-pitched squalls drowning out the quiet rustling of the leaves. Bats even feed on the leaves of the tree when food is scarce.

The peepul is truly a people's tree. It is a source of food, medicine and raw material, worshipped by people, purifies the air and protects a number of other species, from birds to monkeys. Given how long it lives, having a peepul tree in a city is a wonderful thing. After all, the tree can be a constant companion in our ever-changing cities, sharing our lives, those of our children, and their children in turn.

Peepul (*Ficus religiosa*)

Description: A large tree, dome-shaped with a short, thick trunk and shallow grooves (fluted); brownish-grey bark that turns rough as the tree ages.
Flowers: Tiny flowers enclosed within the fruits (figs).
Fruits: Figs are green initially, then turn red and finally blue-black when they ripen.
Leaves: A dark, glossy green. Heart-shaped with acutely pointed tip and wavy margins.
Seasonality: Deciduous tree whose leaves fall in November and December, sometimes extending into January, leaving the tree bare. Figs ripen in April and May.
Family: Moraceae. Plants of this family contain milky latex.
Origin and distribution: Native to India and found throughout the country in its cities, villages and forests.

NINETEEN

TREE-
DEFICIT DISORDER

We live in an increasingly virtual world. Our children, especially those between nine and eleven years of age, spend close to two hours a day in front of a screen, and one in three children may even exceed this. Screen time is harmful for children in many ways, increasing hyperactivity and mental and physical disorders. We may soon end up like the USA, where the average citizen spends more than ten hours before a screen daily, but less than twenty minutes on exercise. It is not surprising that stress and lifestyle disorders such as high blood pressure and diabetes are on the rise.

One of the simplest ways to deal with this is to get outdoors. However, in our polluted and traffic-plagued cities, this is easier said than done. No longer can children go around freely and play on the roads — if they are not exposed to the dangers of traffic, they are certainly breathing in heavily polluted air. The best remedy is to find a green spot, such as a lake or a park, and play a game of cricket or settle down to a family picnic under the shade of a tree. This is stress relief of the most obvious and least expensive kind, but it is something that is becoming increasingly rare in our cities today.

Trees and green spaces encourage exercise and daily activity — the further away we live from them, the more likely we are to be obese, sedentary and suffer from diseases such as circulatory disorders (including high blood pressure) and asthma, as well as stress-related mental health disorders.

Most religions across the world recognize the importance of trees. In some parts of the world, a special day is set aside every year to spend time with trees. In India, many Hindus, especially in Maharashtra and Andhra Pradesh, conduct a *vanabhojana* (a meal amidst trees) each year during Karthika Masam (a month in the Hindu calendar that typically falls between October and November). Families congregate in a park or a forest area, worship a tree (amla trees are considered highly auspicious) by walking around it, winding a sacred thread around it and anointing its bark with haldi and kumkum, after which they settle down to enjoy their picnic lunch. It is a way of paying respect to nature and seeking her blessings. Many memorable Eid picnics have also been held under the welcoming shade of a tree in the park, bringing entire communities together. In Japan, the centuries-old tradition of *hanami* brings together thousands of people who gather under cherry blossom or plum trees to welcome the spring, hosting day-long or even night-long parties.

Recreation in nature helps us relax, makes us creative, gives us energy and improves blood circulation and health, and helps us reconnect with friends, neighbours and family. We may stop to have a quick chat with a friend or eat an afternoon meal under the shade of a tree. Construction workers tie a sari to a branch, creating a sheltered cradle for their sleeping infants while they toil in the sun. A common sight today, delivery boys sit under a tree while waiting for their next order, while Ola and Uber cab drivers park in the shade of a tree while waiting for their next booking.

Many Americans spend 90 per cent of their time inside buildings — many of us in cities and elsewhere are fast reaching this point, especially if we factor in the time spent stuck in traffic. Yet, over evolutionary timescales, we are most 'at home' in natural environments, where we thrived for millenniums. Living in artificial, concrete environments is unnatural for many and brings with it a psychological sense of unease. Contact with trees releases the pressure valve of stress that builds up in city residents.

Environmental psychologists, who have studied how trees help reduce stress, suggest two possible reasons for this. Stress-reduction theory suggests that places of nature help calm us down after a period of intense stress, an automatic subconscious response due to the fact that some natural spaces, such as those with complex elements or with a depth of view, may have been places of plentiful food, or safe spaces where predators could be easily observed and evaded in our evolutionary past, hence places where stress and negative thoughts quickly diminished. Another theory, the attention restoration theory, also relates the importance of nature to our evolutionary past, saying that places of nature are 'inherently intriguing', drawing our attention, and therefore reducing our focus on aspects of life that stress us. Interestingly, studies show that trees are one component of an ideal green space, which should also comprise some place for grass, herbs and shrubs. Too many trees planted close to each other can sometimes present a threatening appearance and even pose real problems, such as security concerns, in places that have high crime rates. Trees, just like pills, are not a panacea for all ills of urban life, but they can certainly help in many ways.

American journalist Robert Louv was one of the first to highlight the importance of places of nature in cities. He pointed out that the lack of contact with nature makes children depressed and solitary, reduces their creativity and increases the chances of health disorders linked to obesity. Louv called this the nature-deficit disorder. Many scientific studies have shown that contact with nature helps prevent depression and improves well-being. A study in the Australian city of Brisbane found that visiting green spaces, for a time as short as half an hour each week reduced the chances of depression by 7 per cent, and high blood pressure by 9 per cent. Inspired by other research showing similar outcomes, the United Kingdom's wildlife trusts have been running a large-scale campaign each year called '30 Days Wild'. They ask people to engage with nature for a month, giving them ideas of activities through apps and local campaigns across the country. Begun in 2015, the campaign now has tens of thousands of participants signing up each year, with people reporting that they feel much happier, healthier, and connected to nature after they participate.

Patients in hospitals who are fortunate to have a window with the view of a tree recover faster and with fewer complications. Not just this, but a location next to a park or tree-lined lake or avenue raises the price of a property. When we visit a wooded grove, we experience a sense of escape from the city and feel as though we are entering a haven. This lowers blood pressure and offers relief from stress-induced disorders such as anxiety and palpitations. Award-winning ecologist E.O. Wilson described this as biophilia — the innate human tendency to seek out nature. We can see this clearly in the company of children, including those with attention-deficit disorders, who often seem calmer, happier and more relaxed in the company of nature.

Experiments have shown that people who exercise in natural surroundings with trees enjoy greater health benefits than those who exercise in indoor gyms or on concrete roads without trees.

The Japanese approach of nature therapy — *Shinrin-yoku* or forest bathing — which became popular in the 1980s, is believed to have all kinds of health effects, from reducing blood pressure and stress to improving sleep, strengthening friendships and increasing happiness and well-being. A study in the USA by Bin Jiang and other scientists from the University of Illinois at Urbana-Champaign and the University of Hong Kong found that, after experiencing stress, when a number of adults were asked to view three-dimensional videos of tree-lined streets, they used words such as 'relaxing, calming, tranquil, at ease, comfortable, peaceful, serene, settled, safe, quiet, a reprieve, mesmerizing, soothing, pleasant, unrushed, undisturbed, enjoyable and worry-free' to describe their experience. If a video could inspire such feelings, it is no surprise that the real experience would be even more transformative.

We do not need to only seek out forests. Parks and wooded streets can also help relieve stress, not to mention that they also offer opportunities for interaction with others. In informal settlements and slums, where people live in congested environments and open space and tree cover are sparse, even a solitary tree can be a hot spot for social interaction, where women chat and groom each other, keeping an eye on their children playing nearby. At other times of the day, men take over in groups, lounging comfortably against the tree trunks. Tree-lined roads are also beehives of social activity, much more in India than in the USA. A study by K.C. Malhotra and Vijaya Kumar found that a 4.6-km stretch on the Barrackpore Trunk Road in Kolkata had 400 trees in 1986. These supported 205 different kinds of activities. Banyan, peepul and neem were places of worship, while large trees provided shade for rickshaw pullers, cart and tempo drivers. Street vendors sold a range of vegetables, fruits and other products here. Cobblers, barbers, tailors and mini-garages operated here too, while vendors supplied tea and food. Trees planted along streets provide direct sources of income too, especially with species like the *Bauhinia*, whose scattered seeds are collected by domestic workers and sold to nurseries, or the Indian beech, whose seeds are made into lamp oil in home industries. Tamarind trees along the road are a favourite with small boys who compete to see who can aim best with a stone and bring down the choicest fruit. Small children are also experts in scaling the wall to climb up mango trees within private or public compounds, deftly getting their hands on the raw fruit which is then chopped, mixed with salt and chilli powder, and eaten with relish as a pickle.

Have you noticed the variety of advertisements that are displayed on trees? Sometimes it is a simple A4 sheet pasted, but at other times it could be a larger flex banner hammered on to the tree—damaging the bark. These posters carry advertisements for paying guest accommodations, contact details of agents who can help with PAN cards and passports, and succinctly communicate messages such as 'meals ready'. In some cases, post boxes are suspended from the trees. While we may stop to drop a letter into the box—an admittedly rare event today—we rarely pay attention to the tree that supports it.

The raised platforms built around sacred trees serve a rich mix of social, spiritual, economic and cultural uses. Worshipped by many, these trees are also places for vendors to congregate with plastic knick-knacks, flowers and fruits, and even pirated DVDs. In the afternoon, we can even see people catching a quick nap in the shade. In the evening, the same space becomes a place for the older residents to collect for lengthy discussions. These platforms also have remnant structures, showing us how they were used in the years gone past. In Karnataka, many such platforms contain small stone receptacles for water, called *sisandra*s. Local residents kept these tanks filled with water for travellers, an old tradition that some residents are now trying to revive.

Trees also act as a rallying point for collective action in a fragmented city, bringing together people from different parts of the city and even different walks of life. In Bengaluru and New Delhi, Salem and Chandigarh, citizens have come together to fight the felling of trees, forming networks that then take on other civic tasks such as waste segregation and civic planning. Research in American cities such as Chicago shows that neighbourhoods with trees have fewer crimes. A number of civic organizations have taken up this finding and begun to plant trees and create community parks in high-crime inner-city neighbourhoods, finding a drop in crime rate and improved safety. Urban festivals recognize the power of trees and celebrate them through tree walks and other activities. Neralu, a crowd-funded Bengaluru tree festival, regularly organizes talks around nature, guided walks in green spaces and activities such as tree sensing and storytelling to help create a stronger connection between people and trees. The iconic Kala Ghoda festival in Mumbai organizes tree walks while in Delhi regular guided walks are conducted in the Aravalli forests.

There is much interest today in trying to understand whether greenery in cities, including trees, can contribute to social cohesion and bringing together people from different backgrounds. The kind of trees we plant can contribute to these exchanges. The peepul is an excellent choice, sacred for both the poor and rich alike. Trees rich with blossoms are a visual treat for the senses. Women, in specific, may prefer particular kinds of trees — for example, the drumstick pods and leaves — as a source of food, used to make curries or added to dal and chapattis — and ficus for shade to carry out mundane household tasks like cooking and washing clothes. Many inner-city neighbourhoods dislike trees like Indian beech or jamun whose fruits fall on and stain vehicles. Planting trees in cities is mostly a human exercise. Perhaps with the correct choice of species we can rid our cities of the tree-deficit disorder, making them not just greener, but also friendlier and more social spaces. Spaces which we live in and not just exist in.

TWENTY

DRUM ROLL FOR
THE DRUMSTICK

Is it just a tree? Or is it a superfood?
Wait! It's the drumstick.

Our neighbourhood tree, a familiar sight in our backyards, the humble drumstick is today touted as a superfood worldwide. In India, we are most familiar with the pods of the fruit, the drum 'stick', from which the tree gets its name. Different parts of the tree have found their way into our diet and lives since historical times. Kings and queens as far back as 150 BC included the drumstick in their diets for improved mental and physical health. One fascinating story says that the undefeated army of Alexander the Great finally met its match in the Mauryan warriors who were fed an extract of the drumstick leaf. The extract kept them free of the stress and pain brought on by the war, enabling them to beat the invading Greek army.

The scientific name, *Moringa oleifera*, comes from its Tamil name *murungai* (which means twisted, referring to the drumstick pod). The species name *oleifera* means that it is oil producing. The origins of its scientific name, and its popularity in south India, give us the impression that the tree originated there. Interestingly, though, the drumstick is native to the southern Himalayas, from where it spread across the Indian subcontinent and beyond. Sambhar (a lentil-based dish) is a staple in almost every south Indian meal. The dish can be made using a combination of vegetables. But whether it is in the high-rise apartments or in the slums, one vegetable that regularly finds its way into the sambhar is the drumstick. The leaves of the tree can also be roasted and added to this dish. This makes sense. Long before the tree was touted as a modern superfood, India knew much about its nutritional and medicinal value.

The drumstick tree is a powerhouse of vitamins, minerals and amino acids. A study by the National Institute of Nutrition in Hyderabad found that it has seven times more vitamin C than oranges, fifteen times more potassium than bananas, ten times more vitamin A than carrots and twenty-five times more iron than spinach. It also has seventeen times more calcium than milk and nine times more protein than curd. Small wonder then that the drumstick is also called a 'mother's best friend'. Nursing mothers eat the leaves to help increase milk production. The tiny white flowers of the tree, which appear in clusters twice or thrice a year, are also used in cooking. A paste of drumstick leaves can be applied on the skin to reduce pain and swelling. The oil from its seeds is used to make soaps, cosmetics and perfumes.

The root of the drumstick has a pungent taste, similar to that of the horseradish, which is why it is also called the horseradish tree. It turned out to be a boon for British cooks who struggled to replicate the taste of their English sauces in India. They peeled and dried the roots, and mixed them with vinegar to use as garnish. Wyvern (Colonel Arthur Robert Kenny-Herbert) in his 1880 book *Culinary Jottings for Madras* described how the drumstick roots could be used as a substitute for horseradish. He said, 'Scrape as finely as you can a cupful of the root shavings, simmer them in half a pint of chicken broth; when done, thicken the broth custard-wise with the yolks of three eggs beaten up with a dessert spoonful of tarragon vinegar; add pepper, salt, and a very little grated nutmeg, and serve in a sauce-boat.' Colonel Kenny-Herbert also suggested that tender drumstick pods be used in a recipe for topping of toast. The common man's drumstick thus made its way into the multi-course meals of the British in India.

Despite the many uses of this miracle tree, it does not look very imposing. In fact, it looks bedraggled compared to trees we see in cities, such as the rain tree. The drumstick belongs to the Moringaceae family. It is fast-growing and can quickly reach a height of 10–15 metres. It is a hardy tree that can survive in both wet and dry climates, it grows in poor soil and even in tiny spaces. These qualities make it a popular tree in many congested inner parts of cities, such as Bengaluru's Chickpet area, where people plant it in their backyards. The only thing to watch out for is the ever-present *murangamara kamblipoochi* (the drumstick blanket worm), the brown and bristly caterpillars of the *Eupterote mollifera* moth. If these brush against your skin or fall on you, you are in for hours of intense itching and pain.

Drumstick trees are also popular in slums. Long before the drumstick was recognized as a superfood, families living in slums used the leaves and pods in their meals. For women, on whose shoulders the daily task of cooking and providing a healthy meal falls, the drumstick is of help in meeting the hunger and nutritional needs of their families. Women living in slums also come up with different arrangements to share the pods and leaves among themselves, to ensure that there is food for all, without fights.

Today, there is an increasing number of movements to plant drumstick trees in schools and *anganwadi*s (childcare centres) to feed children and address malnutrition. A single tree can supply a large number of pods that can be added to the midday meal. Of course, getting children to eat the pods is another challenge altogether. Some children enjoy crushing the boiled pods in their mouth and sucking on the fibre, while others gag on them because of the slimy texture. The leaves are excellent sources of vitamins, but young children may find them difficult to digest. In South Africa, porridge with drumstick powder is now being introduced in some communities. There are complaints though that this adds a bitter taste and changes the smell and taste of the traditional maize porridge. Mothers, however, are willing to try it to give their children better food. We too need to think of ingenious ways of using the drumstick in our anganwadis.

Another use of this miracle tree is to purify polluted water in cities. Women in Sudan use an extract of the dried seed instead of alum to treat turbid water. In fact, the tree is also called *Shagara al Rauwaq* (the tree of purification) in the Nile Valley. The dried and ground drumstick seeds have similar coagulation properties as that of alum but are healthier. The seeds are also antiseptic and antimicrobial, treating the water as well as precipitating out the murky material from it.

Hunger, malnutrition and polluted water are huge challenges facing the poor in Indian cities. Encouraging the planting of drumstick trees can help address many of these problems. The economic capital of India, Mumbai, has some of the highest levels of child hunger. In the early 1900s, the city had a large number of drumstick trees whose pods were collected and sold in local markets. Maybe it is time to re-green Mumbai's landscape, and those of other cities, with the drumstick that was once so common? The drumstick has fans outside India too.

Cuba's former prime minister and president, the iconic Fidel Castro, is said to have been a big fan of the drumstick. He, in fact, planted several trees in his backyard. The tree was originally brought to Cuba from Brazil by Castro's comrade, the equally iconic revolutionary Che Guevara (whom we see on T-shirts across India) in the 1960s. But of the sixteen seeds that Guevara brought, only one is said to have survived. The drumstick that Castro planted in his house was brought more recently in 2010, from Kerala and Tamil Nadu, when Castro discovered its medicinal and nutritional properties and got 100 tonnes of seeds shipped to Cuba.

There is a saying in Tamil: *vethalam pinnayum muringa marathil*. Literally translated, this means 'running behind the ghost while forgetting the drumstick tree', which refers to running after an illusion while forgetting the thing of utmost importance. The phrase is taken from the famous stories about the legendary King Vikramaditya's encounters with a wily vethalam (ghost) who hangs upside down from a drumstick tree located in a cemetery. To fulfil a promise made to a magician, the king attempts to capture the ghost. Each time, the ghost tricks him with a story and escapes, returning to the topmost branch of the tree. The folk saying remains apt even today. While the world is turning back to the drumstick and food stores across the country are offering bottled drumstick powder, we seem to have forgotten the importance of this once-common tree. It is time to raise a drum roll for the drumstick, plant it in the nooks, crannies and corners of our streets and backyards, and include the pods, leaves and flowers of the miracle tree in our daily diet.

Drumstick (*Moringa oleifera*)

Description: Medium-sized tree with a light crown. Pale brown bark with deep fissures.

Flowers: Small yellowish-white flowers that grow in clusters.

Fruits: Green, ribbed, long stick-like pods hanging downward; within the pods are winged seeds in a fleshy pulp.

Leaves: Leathery small leaves that are elliptical in shape.

Seasonality: Deciduous with leaves turning yellow and falling in December and January. Flowering is between January and March. Fruits ripen between April and January.

Family: Moringaceae. Only a single genus, *Moringa*, is included in this family.

Origin and distribution: Native to India.

TWENTY-ONE

TREES
OF RECIPES
AND REMEDIES

A young child is taught early on in school that the food she eats is produced by farmers and that medicines can be bought from pharmacies. But how many of us see the trees in our towns and cities as sources of food and medicine?

Many people from the older generations have memories of using the trees that grow around them for food and medicine. Today, this knowledge has largely faded from our collective memory, except perhaps for migrant labourers from distant villages who bring with them the knowledge about different trees and plants as sources of food and medicine, or the residents of erstwhile villages that are engulfed by cities. The rest of us, the city dwellers, never really view trees through this lens.

We are of course familiar with the uses of some common trees. The tamarind is a hardy tree with many uses, but it is primarily planted for its fruit whose pulp is commonly used in cooking. It is mostly bought from stores these days, but children still gather under these trees to pluck and suck on the green or semi-ripe pods.

It may be difficult for us to imagine now, but during the grain crisis in India in the 1950s, tamarind kernel powder (or TKP as it was known) was once considered as a subsidiary food. The Government of India was spending crores of rupees on importing foodgrains. Concerned that the crisis may worsen, scientists began to explore alternative options. Tamarind kernel seeds, a well-known source of food, were consumed mainly during times of famine. But that is not to say that they weren't eaten at other times. The powder was used to make laddoos or mixed with other kinds of flour to make chapattis. These seeds came with the added benefit of possessing medicinal properties and were used in Ayurveda and Unani medicine.

Other common fruiting trees sighted on Indian streets are the jamun, mango and star gooseberry. Purplish tongues are signs of afternoons well spent under a jamun tree. Bringing down a mango with a well-aimed shot is as satisfying as eating it with some salt and chilli powder. Mangoes seem to taste even better if the process of plucking them involves being chased by cantankerous owners of the house in whose compound the tree stands. Some old mango trees still line the streets in cities, but few children have the time to climb it — and neither is it safe given the traffic. The other fruit is the star gooseberry, which is different from the more common amla. The fruits of the star gooseberry grow close to the branches of the tree in bunches. They can be eaten fresh, plucked right from the tree, with a pinch of salt. They can also be pickled.

Coconut and drumstick trees are important for the flavours and nutrition they add to our daily diets. Neem flowers are used in cooking for the bitter flavour they impart, believed to help in digestion and in treating stomach disorders. Bengalis sprinkle neem flowers, roasted with ghee, on their bhajas and poshtos, while in south India chutneys are made from neem flowers or added to rasam. The dried flowers can also be mixed with rice and ghee and eaten, though this is an acquired taste. Shops in cities also sell dried neem flowers. Slums are a microcosm of the city. For women who must feed their families and growing children on tight budgets, trees like the drumstick and coconut, which grow in confined spaces, are very important to supplement their nutrition.

Flowers of the banana are widely used in cooking. Cooking with flowers may be a fad today, making appearances in upmarket restaurants in dishes prepared by gourmet chefs. But other flowers, less known than the banana flower, have been mentioned as ingredients in ancient books such as the *Lokapakara, Ni'matnama* and *Supashastra*. Flowers of common avenue trees such as mango, ironwood, champaka and palmyra are mentioned as being cooked with vegetables and different kinds of meat. Children love to eat the striped part of the gulmohar flower that lies at its centre, which has a characteristic sour taste. The buds of the silk-cotton and orchid trees are relished in meat and vegetable dishes.

Some seeds also make it to our tables. The jackfruit has recently been in the news as a superfruit, touted for its ability to tackle the food and nutritional problems of the developing world. The seeds are incredibly tasty when roasted or steamed. Once viewed as a poor man's food, people are now waking up to the nutritional benefits of its seeds. The jackfruit is now popularized by animal rights groups, who see its texture as a substitute for meat, used in restaurants to make pulled jackfruit tacos and other meat substitutes. PETA (People for the Ethical Treatment of Animals) even named the jackfruit as the hottest food trend in 2017. Another common city tree, the cluster fig, is also becoming popular in everyday cooking, with a number of recipes being shared by chefs and homemakers for dishes ranging from kebabs to vegetable curries and fries. Figs are power-packed centres of nutrition, dense with calories and fibre and particularly sought after by diabetics and the elderly.

Another very valuable tree is the mahua, whose flowers and fruits are used as food. The mahua is of great importance for the poor in India, who depend on its flowers and fruits as a source of food, while oil is extracted from its seeds. The flower is especially sought-after; it is collected, sun-dried and stored to be eaten throughout the year. In the forests of central India, a host of animals and birds feast on its flowers. The flowers can also be distilled to produce a fermented intoxicating brew that is known to make both humans and bears dance. This potent brew was even exported to France in the early 1900s, with the hope that it would sell like French brandy, but the French government put a stop to it.

While the mahua is a tree that most associate with the forest, solitary specimens are found in temples, along roads and even in the urban groves of Bengaluru. Pradip Krishen, in *Trees of Delhi* bemoans the fact that a tree of such value can be found only on one avenue in the national capital. Similarly, a variety of fruit trees that grew in abundance in our cities seem to have been lost over time. Some of the most widely planted fruit trees in Mumbai in 1909 included pomelo, wood apple, bael, mango, cashew, hog plum, jackfruit and breadfruit. These trees are rare in the city today.

Many trees are especially valued for their medicinal uses. The devil's tree, planted in many parks, is held in awe. Many believe that spirits reside in the leaves of this tree, and once every year, the other trees come to pay homage to it. The dark grey, rough bark of this tree is considered a powerful tonic. The Tulu and Konkani communities extract a bitter juice from the bark that is forced into the mouths of all family members during the lunar month of Aati as it is believed to ward off all stomach disorders.

Many of the common trees in our cities have a range of medicinal properties and are used in home remedies, as well as in Ayurveda, Unani and Siddha. Extracts from leaves, fruits, flowers, seeds and bark have been prescribed for a wide range of ailments, from a simple headache to leprosy. There is a saying in Tamil about the banyan, *aalum velum pallukkurudhi* (both the twig of the banyan and the Arabian gum tree give strength to the teeth). The use of the banyan is not limited to just cleaning teeth. A member of a community of bamboo weavers who dwell on the pavement in Bengaluru told us how the milky sap from the tree was extracted by making a cut in the bark and mixed with day-old balls of ragi (finger millet) and swallowed in the morning to treat coughs. A simple but effective cure, according to him, it saved his parents from many a visit to the doctors, which they could barely afford to pay for. These trees have long been cut down to make way, first for widening the road and then for the metro. The weavers have lost not only the shade of the trees but also their free roadside 'medical store'.

The fruit of the mango — the king of fruits — takes our focus away from the other parts of the tree. But the leaves of the mango produce a compound called mangiferin which has a number of useful properties, including being antimicrobial, anticancer, antioxidant, and having the potential to reduce diabetes and cholesterol levels. Decoctions and concoctions made from different parts of the tree are believed to have various health benefits. Then there are the more exotic stories one hears about its healing powers. Balwant Singh, a former conservator of forests in Chamba, Himachal Pradesh, wrote in the *Indian Forester* in 1951 that he once saw an advocate friend relieve a child of the pain of a wasp bite. The forester repeatedly asked the advocate what charm the latter had used to soothe the crying child. The advocate responded, 'Take some inflorescence of mango, before it is ripe, rub it between your hands and let it dry. Try it three to four times again on subsequent days. It will impart to your hands the charm exhibited by me.' The forester claimed that he tested the efficacy of this method and found that it worked. Just by rubbing his hands three to four times with the flowers, he claimed, he found that his hands retained their healing property as long as a year later, until the next flowering season.

There are many myths and legends about the uses of trees, and some facts intermingled with fiction. Champaka flowers can reduce fevers, cluster fig flowers and bark are used to treat urinary infections and coconut milk can relieve intestinal ulcers. The list of medicinal uses of trees is endless. While they may not provide a cure for more complicated or fatal diseases, they can definitely provide relief from minor ailments and infections.

We know that the trees we see in our cities provide shade, clean up pollution and are pleasing to the eye. But they are also a source of food and nature's own pharmacies, an essential fact that is now fading from our consciousness. Cities such as San Francisco and New York now have communities of urban foragers who teach others about what food can be collected and consumed safely from plants and trees in the city, and what to avoid. In Kampala, Uganda, surveys conducted in 2015 by researchers found that half of the city's low-income residents collect wild plants to consume as food and medicine. Celebrity chefs in many cities now advertise the joys of cooking with freshly plucked edible wild food from the city. A growing number of crowd-sourced maps also exist, pointing both novices and experts towards food sources in American and European cities. 'Delhi, I Love You', a movement aimed at helping residents reconnect to their city, took people on a walk in Lodhi Gardens, helping them identify and collect edible plants, which they later cooked and ate. It would be wonderful to recreate such efforts in India, helping to revive these memories of a way of urban living in harmony with our edible environment.

Hair Oil with Amla, Curry Leaves and Banyan Roots

Ingredients:

- Half a litre of hair oil of your choice (coconut or sesame)
- 100 gram amla fruits
- One cup tightly packed curry leaves
- A handful of tender banyan roots

Method:

Wash the amla, curry leaves and banyan roots. Pat them dry with a towel and spread them out on a newspaper or a clean towel. Dry them indoors for a few hours until no moisture remains on the surface. Roughly chop the roots into small pieces, using sharp scissors. Chop the amla as well and remove the seeds. (You can roughly pound the fruit into small pieces using a mortar and pestle to remove the seeds if that is easier for you than trying to cut the fruit).

Heat a heavy-bottomed steel or iron pan for two to three minutes. Add the oil to the hot pan. Heat it for a few minutes on a moderate flame (as you would heat oil for deep-frying puris, for example) until it is close to boiling — ensure the oil does not begin to smoke. Test the temperature by adding a single curry leaf — it should sizzle and splutter.

Once the oil has reached the desired temperature, add the chopped amla, banyan roots and curry leaves. Be sure to stand away from the vessel as you do this, as the oil will splutter and can fall on you. Once these ingredients are added, the oil will come to a boil and bubbles will form on the surface. Turn the heat down to medium and cook for fifteen to twenty minutes, until the excess moisture is removed and the curry leaves begin to turn brown.

Turn off the heat and remove the saucepan to a cool and dry location. Leave the vessel uncovered until the oil cools down completely. This can take a few hours. Then cover the vessel with a plate and set aside for three days. Strain the oil using a cheesecloth and discard the solid material. This oil can be stored for several months and used daily or weekly to oil your scalp. It is also excellent for a hot-oil scalp massage, after which it can be left to soak for an hour and then washed off. In south India, it is believed that these ingredients are excellent for stimulating hair growth, preventing premature greying and reducing dandruff.

TWENTY-TWO

WHAT
LIES AHEAD?

Tall or wide, spreading or stunted, flowering or bare-branched, trees support birds, insects, squirrels and many other varieties of life, both noisy and silent. It is because of trees that we can survive in cities; we may not have enough oxygen to breathe otherwise. They cool the city, clean up polluted air, aid rainfall and provide food for people and animals.

But trees are much more than just the purposes they serve. They are creatures of our imagination. Trees are a well-known part of our most-loved books. Those who have read Shel Silverstein's poignant children's book, *The Giving Tree*, or Shivaram Karanth's *Mookajjiya Kanasugalu*, with its layered conversations between a grandmother and her grandson under the shade of a ficus tree, cannot help but think of the tree as a character with feelings and personalities that are central to the story. When trees are in danger of being cut for a new road or a building, people tie sacred threads around them and hug them. Inspired by the Chipko and Appiko community forest protection movements, they form human chains to protect the trees. Some people even name the trees in their backyards and spend hours talking to them.

But not all trees are considered benevolent and friendly. Some species are associated with ghosts and evil spirits. In times of war—such as the 1857 revolt in Delhi—sepoys used the trees for protection while firing at the British. Once the mutiny was quashed, all the trees in a 500-yard radius around Delhi were cut down and the buildings razed, to provide a clean (and safe) line of sight. Dense clumps of trees are disliked even today in many parts of the city, but for different reasons. As per surveys conducted in Bengaluru, people tend to prefer parks with some trees, but not too many—walking into a densely wooded park or plantation brings a sense of unease, of being unsafe, especially for women and children. Visibility is the key to safety in our cities, even in public spaces. This contradiction has been pointed out by many planners and researchers. We want trees around us because we feel more natural, intimate and at home with them. Yet we fear trees because of their wildness, unpredictability and lack of control. The darkness seems to hide much. Dense, green patches assume spooky and sinister connotations. Instinctively, many of us tend to avoid such places, especially if we are alone, and even more so if we feel vulnerable (as many women, young children and the elderly tend to).

Some say our complex association with trees can be linked to our evolutionary history. The earliest humans evolved in a world filled with trees. Forests were places of danger where you couldn't see what was behind the nearest tree. It was likely to be something dangerous—a snake, a beehive or a tiger. Areas without trees were either too cold or too hot and often too dry for us to be comfortable in, or to provide enough food and water for us. Savanna-like landscapes with some trees—enough to provide food but not too many, so we could have a clear line of sight—were the places that early humans were believed to have spent most time in.

This theory is controversial and not all place their faith in it. Also, just like each tree is different from its neighbour, so are we. Some of us may be most at home in isolated, wooded groves, without finding them creepy in the slightest. Others may prefer more landscaped parks. Migrant workers living in tents in a grove may have a very different opinion on what they would like, compared to cattle grazers who bring their cows to forage under the trees. Whatever your needs and preferences, a city should have space for everyone to find a spot with the trees that they like, which provides them with what they need and where they can feel at home. At least, that is the dream.

The reality is quite different, of course. Rarely are we, the people who live in cities, consulted by planners and developers. They decide on the fate of plants and trees with one eye at checklists and budgets, models and paper sketches, while they should also consider traipsing around on two feet, asking people how they would like to live. When planners or developers do talk to people, they restrict themselves to only some kinds of people. Rarely do they consult the majority of those who live in the city — in shanties, in small homes, walking on hot treeless streets, living on the margins and depending on trees as screens behind which they can bathe or use as a toilet, for food, firewood and medicines that supplement what they cannot afford to buy.

We often go about our daily lives without giving much thought to the trees we see around us. A number of initiatives, in India and outside, are trying to change this. Tree walks are now held in dozens of cities across India. Experienced naturalists take people on trails in the heart of their city, helping them discover a world of trees, spiders, butterflies, birds and other fascinating creatures that they had never looked at, but suddenly seem to be everywhere.

Tree whisperers help us get in touch with trees, thereby enabling us to reconnect with ourselves.

Interest in citizen science is increasing as well, with people beginning to get involved in science research. The Urban Slender Loris Project in Bengaluru helps train people to look for the endangered, shy animal in the city. The eBird app began to be used by birdwatchers in India to record birds in early 2014. By the end of 2016, there were more than four million observations of over 1200 species across the country. This data can be used to track if waterbirds are deserting Indian cities as the lakes and rivers dry up. It can also be used to study whether the appearance of the pied cuckoo in different parts of India tracks the monsoon, as our oral traditions say they do.

The nationwide programme SeasonWatch asks people to select a tree, observe it through the year and note when new flowers, fruits and leaves appear. Individually, this is a fun exercise to do that helps you get to know a tree better. Collectively, the programme now has information on close to 25,000 trees (many from Kerala, where a large number of schools participate in it). They can now use this data to answer interesting questions like the effect of global warming on the timing of tree flowering. Individual scientists cannot collect data on such a big scale. But we need to know the answers, if we are to make our cities more resilient to climate change. A useful outcome is that people become much more attached to the trees they monitor, helping treat them if they are diseased and to protect them when they are threatened. A childhood pastime can turn into a life-changing activity.

Other programmes such as Inside Wood, a website run by North Carolina State University, may not help us get outside, but can certainly satisfy our curiosity about parts of the tree we don't normally get a chance to see. As the name suggests, this website helps you peer inside trees to see how the wood looks. The website has more than 40,000 photos of slices of wood taken from 200 families of trees, including fossilized trees from the hoary past, as well as the insides of modern-day trees that we see around us today. It is interesting to see the various patterns and shapes that cells inside the wood take. You can guess and see if you are able to identify different types of trees based on these internal patterns, like the specialists do.

Trees in Indian cities are an infinite topic, endlessly engrossing. There are many more interesting activities and resources that we simply do not have space to cover. This is an idiosyncratic account, featuring some of our favourites. Whether on your phone or with a paper and pencil in hand, we hope these resources help you explore the trees in your city from a different perspective. And we hope that you will share with us stories and histories of trees in the cities that you live in, including smaller towns and parts of India that we are not very familiar with. We look forward to hearing from you. You can write to us at treesofindiancities@gmail.com with recipes, games, stories and pointers that you would like to share and those which can add to our own knowledge.

SCIENTIFIC NAMES
OF TREES

Acacia: *Acacia sp.*
African tulip: *Spathodea campanulata*
Amaltas: *Cassia fistula*
Amla: *Phyllanthus emblica*
Ashoka: *Saraca asoca*
Australian black wattle: *Acacia mearnsii*
Bael: *Aegle marmelos*
Balsam fir: *Abies balsamea*
Banyan: *Ficus benghalensis*
Baobab: *Adansonia digitata*
Ber: *Ziziphus mauritiana*
Betel nut palm: *Areca catechu*
Bidi leaf tree: *Bauhinia racemosa*
Big-leaved mahogany: *Swietenia macrophylla*
Bilwa: see bael
Blue gum: *Eucalyptus tereticornis*
Breadfruit: *Artocarpus altilis*

Brown top: *Eucalyptus obliqua*
Buddha coconut: *Pterygota alata*
Cannonball tree: *Couroupita guianensis*
Cashew: *Anacardium occidentale*
Casuarina: *Casuarina equisetifolia*
Ceibo: see kapok
Cinchona: *Cinchona officinalis*
Champaka: *Magnolia champaca*
Cherry blossom: *Prunus sp.*
Chinar: *Platanus orientalis*
Cluster fig: *Ficus racemosa*
Coconut: *Cocos nucifera*
Copper pod: *Peltophorum pterocarpum*
Date palm: *Phoenix sylvestris*
Douglas fir: *Pseudotsuga menziesii var. glauca*
Drumstick: *Moringa oleifera*
False hemp tree: *Tetrameles nudiflora*
Fig: *Ficus sp.*
Fir: *Abies sp.*
Fishtail palm: *Caryota urens*
Frangipani: *Plumeria sp.*
Guava: *Psidium guajava*
Gulmohar: *Delonix regia*
Hog plum: *Spondias mombin*
Indian beech: *Pongamia pinnata (syn. Milletia pinnata)*
Indian mast tree: *Polyalthia longifolia*
Ironwood: *Senna siamea*
Jacaranda: *Jacaranda mimosifolia*
Jackfruit: *Artocarpus heterophyllus*
Jamun: *Syzygium cumini*
Kapok: *Ceiba pentandra*

Khirni: *Manilkara hexandra*
Lemon-scented gum: *Eucalyptus citriodora* (now called *Corymbia citriodora*)
Mahua: *Madhuca longifolia*
Mango: *Mangifera indica*
Mesquite: *Prosopis juliflora*
Mulberry: *Morus serrata*
Mysore fig: *Ficus drupacea*
Neem: *Azadirachta indica*
Oaks: *Quercus sp.*
Olive: *Olea europaea*
Orchid tree: *Bauhinia variegata*
Palash: *Butea monosperma*
Palmyra: *Borassus flabellifer*
Paper birch: *Betula papyrifera*
Peepul: *Ficus religiosa*
Pine: *Pinus sp.*
Pink cassia: *Cassia javanica*
Plum: *Prunus sp.*
Plumeria: see Frangipani
Pomelo: *Citrus grandis*
Ponderosa pine: *Pinus ponderosa*
Poplar: *Populus sp.*
Rain tree: *Samanea saman*
Red sandalwood tree: *Adenanthera pavonina*
Red silk cotton: *Bombax ceiba*
River red gum: *Eucalyptus camaldulensis*
Rose gum: *Eucalyptus grandis*
Royal palm: *Roystonea regia*
Rudraksh: *Elaeocarpus ganitrus*
Sausage tree: *Kigelia africana*

Sea island cotton: *Gossypium barbadense*
Shisham: *Dalbergia sissoo*
Silver oak: *Grevillea robusta*
Shirish: *Albizia lebbeck*
Sitka willow tree: *Salix sitchensis*
Soapnut: *Sapindus emarginatus/Sapindus mukorossi*
South Indian kanak champa: *Pterospermum reticulatum*
Star gooseberry: *Phyllanthus acidus*
Subabul: *Leucaena leucocephala*
Sugar maple: *Acer saccharum*
Swamp mahogany: *Eucalyptus robusta*
Sycamore fig: *Ficus sycomorus*
Talipot palm: *Corypha umbraculifera*
Tamarind: *Tamarindus indica*
Tamarisk: *Tamarisk sp.*
Tasmanian blue gum: *Eucalyptus globulus*
Wild badam: *Sterculia foetida*
Wood apple: see bael

SOURCES

We have avoided citing sources in the text to make the reading experience more enjoyable. Below is a list of sources, including research papers and books. To keep this list manageable, we have avoided listing newspaper and Internet articles from which we may have taken well-known information such as locations of specific trees or descriptions of events.

1.   A Khichri of Trees
i.   Johnston E.H. (translator) (1936), *Buddhacarita* or *Acts of the Buddha* (Part II), Calcutta: Baptist Mission Press, pp: 51.
ii.   Nagendra H., Sudhira H.S., Katti M., Schewenius M. (2013), 'Sub-regional Assessment of India: Effects of Urbanization on Land Use, Biodiversity and Ecosystem Services', *Urbanization, Biodiversity, and Ecosystem Services: Challenges and Opportunities* (eds. Elmqvist T., Fragkias M., Goodness J., et al.) New York, London: Springer; pp. 65–74.
iii. Singh R.K. (1976), 'Cities and Parks in Ancient India', *Ekistics* 42(253): pp. 272–76.

2.   Jamun: The Tree at the Centre of the World
i.   Araga R., Soni S., Sharma C.S. (2017), 'Fluoride Adsorption from Aqueous Solution Using Activated Carbon Obtained

from KOH-treated Jamun (*Syzygium cumini*) Seed', *Journal of Environmental Chemical Engineering* 5: pp. 5608–616.

ii. Ayyanar M., Subash-Babu P. (2012), '*Syzygium cumini* (L.) Skeels: A Review of Its Phytochemical Constituents and Traditional Uses', *Asian Pacific Journal of Tropical Biomedicine* 2(3): pp. 240–46.

iii. Baber, M.Z. (1826), *Memoirs of Zehir-ed-Din Muhammed Baber: Emperor of Hindustan*, written by himself in the Jaghatai Turki and translated partly by late John Leyden and partly by William Erskine with notes and a geographical and historical introduction, Edinburgh: Longman, Rees, Orme, Brown and Green Paternaster Row, and Cadell and Co.

iv. Meister M.W. (2009), 'Exploring Kāfirkot: When Is a Rose Apple Not a Rose', *Pakistan Heritage* 1: pp. 109–28.

v.   Sawhney N., Satapathi S. (2016), 'Utilization of Naturally Occurring Dyes As Sensitizers in Dye-Sensitized Solar Cells', *IEEE Journal of Photovoltaics* 7(2) : pp. 539–44.

vi. Wujastyx D. (2004), 'Jambudvipa: Apples or Plums', *Studies in the History of the Exact Sciences in Honour of David Pingree* (eds. Burnett, et al), Lieden, Boston: Brill.

3. All Creatures Great and Small

i.   'Eha' Aitken E.H. (1904), *The Tribes on My Frontier: Indian Naturalists' Foreign Policy,* London: W. Thacker & Co.

ii. Agoramoorthy G. (2005), 'Disallow Caste Discrimination in Biological and Social Contexts', *Current Science* 89(5): pp. 727.

iii. Das A., Sarkar S., Banerjee K., et al. (2014), 'A Study on the Occurrence of Asia Open Bill Stork, *Anastomus oscitans* in Particular Tree Species at Nature Park, Kolkata, India', *International Letters of Natural Sciences* 22: pp. 19–31.

iv.   eBird, https://ebird.org/home.

v.   India Bird Races, http://indiabirdraces.in/.

vi.   Krishnan M. (2012), *Of Birds and Birdsong* (eds Chandola S., Chandola A), New Delhi: Aleph Book Company.

vii.   Lal R. (2002), *Birds from My Window*, Chennai: Tulika.

viii.   MigrantWatch, www.migrantwatch.in.

ix.   Narendar A., Kumar S. (2006), *On a Trail with Ants: A Handbook of the Ants of Peninsular India*, self-published.

x.   Rajesh T.P., Ballullaya U.P., Surendran P., Sinu P.A. (2017), 'Ants Indicate Urbanization Pressure in Sacred Groves of Southwest India', *Current Science* 113(2): pp. 317–22.

xi.   Roshnath R., Sinu P.A. (2017), 'Nesting Tree Characteristics of Heronry Birds of Urban Ecosystems in Peninsular India: Implications for Habitat Management', *Current Zoology* 63(6): pp. 599–605.

xii.   Turaga J. (2015), 'Birds and Trees in an Urban Context: An Ecosystem Paradigm for Vasant Vihar, New Delhi, India', *Indian Birds* 10(3 and 4): pp. 85–93.

xiii.   Urban Slender Loris Project, www.urbanslenderlorisproject. org.

xiv.   Varghese T. (2006), 'A New Species of the Ant Genus *Dilobocondyla* (Hymenoptera: Formicidae) from India, with Notes on Its Nesting Behaviour', *Oriental Insects* 40: pp. 23–32.

xv.   Wilson E.O. (1984), *Biophilia*, Cambridge: Harvard University Press.

4.   The Shaggy-Headed Banyan Tree

i.   Athreya V.R. (1997), 'Trees with a Difference: Strangler Figs', *Resonance*, July 1997: pp. 67–74.

ii.   Janzen D.H. (1979), 'How to Be a Fig', *Annual Review of Ecological Systems* 10: pp. 13–51.

iii.   Milton J. (1667), *Paradise Lost: A Poem Written in Ten Books*, London: Peter Parker.

iv.   Noehden G.H. (1824), 'Account of the Banyan-Tree, or *Ficus indica*, as Found in the Ancient Greek and Roman', *Transactions of the Royal Asiatic Society of Great Britain and Ireland* 1(1): pp. 119–32.

v.   Parpola A. (2009), '"Hind Leg" + "Fish": Towards Further Understanding of the Indus Script', *Scripta* 1: pp. 37–76.

vi.   Tagore R. (1913), *The Crescent Moon*, translated from the original Bengali by the author with eight illustrations in colour, London and New York: Macmillan and Company.

vii.   Weiblen G.D. (2002), 'How to Be a Fig Wasp', *Annual Review of Entomology* 47: pp. 299–330.

5.   Talking to Trees

i.   Chandi M. (2010), 'Territory and Landscape Around the Jarawa Reserve', *The Jarawa Tribal Reserve Dossier: Cultural and Biological Diversities in the Andaman Islands*, (Sekhsaria P., Pandya V,) Paris: UNESCO.

ii.   Chin K.Y. (2014), 'The Social Life of Plants', ScientEphic: Williams College Science blog, 5 October 2014.

iii.   Gagliano M. (2012), 'Green Symphonies: A Call for Studies on Acoustic Communication in Plants', *Behavioral Ecology* 24(4) pp. 790–96.

iv.   Gagliano M. (2014), 'In a Green Frame of Mind: Perspectives on the Behavioural Ecology and Cognitive Nature of Plants', *AoB Plants* 7: plu075.

v.   Gross M. (2016), 'Could Plants have Cognitive Abilities?', *Current Biology* 26: R181–91.

vi.   Guédon D., 'Chemical Signals As a Means of Communication and Cooperation between Plants', Arkorpharma, https://www.arkopharma.com/en-GB/plant-communication.

vii.   Haskell D.G. (2018), *The Songs of Trees: Stories from Nature's Great Connectors*, New York: Penguin Books.

viii. Karban R., Orrock J.L., Preisser E.L., Sih A. (2016), 'A Comparison of Plants and Animals in Their Responses to Risk of Consumption', *Current Opinion in Plant Biology* 32: pp. 1–8.

ix.   Pollan M. (2013), 'The Intelligent Plant', *New Yorker*, 23 and 30 December 2013.

x.   Popova M. (2015), 'Marianne Moore and the Crowning Curio: How a Poem Saved One of the World's Rarest and Most Majestic Trees', Brainpickings, 13 August 2015.

xi.   Simard S.W. (2018), 'Mycorrhizal Networks Facilitate Tree Communication, Learning, and Memory', *Memory and Learning in Plants: Signaling and Communication in Plants*, (eds. Baluska F., Gagliano M., Witzany G. Cham), Springer, pp. 191–213.

6.   Palms: Superstars or Has-Beens?

i.   Ahuja S.C., Ahuja S., Ahuja U. (2014), 'Coconut: History, Uses and Folklore', *Asian Agri-History* 18(3): pp. 221–48.

ii.   Chang E., Elevitch C.R. (2006), '*Cocos nucifera*', *Species Profile for Pacific Island Agroforestry*.

iii.   Crooke W. (1896), *The Popular Religion and Folk-Lore of Northern India* (vol. II), Westminster: Archibald Constable & Co.

iv.   Curtis Gardners Intelligence Department, 'Nuts and Milk: A Blend of the West of England and Tropics', *The Cult of the Coconut*, pp. 84–86.

v.   Dailey V. (2014), *Piety and Perversity: The Palms of Los Angeles*, Los Angeles Review of Books, 14 July 2014.

vi.   Davis D.A., Johnson D. V. (1987), 'Current Utilization and Further Development of the Palmyra Palm (*Borassus flabellifer* L., Areaceae) in Tamil Nadu State, India', *Economic Botany* 41 (2): pp. 247–66.

vii. Dayrit F.M. (2017), 'Coconut Oil: Bringing History, Common Sense and Science Together', *KIMIKA* 28(2): pp. 55–61.

viii. Douglas J. (1883), *A Book of Bombay: From AD 1661*, Bombay: Bombay Gazette Steam Press.

ix. Edwards S.M. (1909), *The Gazetteer of Bombay City and Island* (vol. I), Bombay: Cosmo Publications.

x. Elwood A.K. (1830), *Narrative of a Journey Overland from England by the Continent of Europe, Egypt and the Red Sea to India, Including a Residence and Voyage Home in the Years 1825, 26, 27 and 28* (vol. 1), London: Henry Colburn and Richard Bentley.

xi. Food and Agriculture Organisation of the United Nations (1995), 'Tropical Palms. No 10, Non-wood Forest Products'.

xii. Ghose S., Tripathi P.K., Sahoo M.C. (2000), 'Coconut in the Folk Culture of Orissa', *Asian Agri-History* 4(2): pp. 143–48.

xiii. Harries C.H., Clement R.C. (2014), 'Long-distance Dispersal of the Coconut Palm by Migration within the Coral Atoll Ecosystem', *Annals of Botany* 113: pp. 565-70.

xiv. Lewandowski S. (2007), 'Urban Planning in the Asia Port City: Madras, An Overview, 1920–1970', South Asia: *Journal of South Asian Studies* 2(1–2): pp. 30–45.

xv. Ohler J.G. (1984), 'Coconut: Tree of life. No 57 FAO Plant Production and Protection Paper', Food and Agriculture Organisation.

xvi. Wallace R.G. (1824) *Memoirs of India: A Brief Geographical Account of the East Indies: A Succinct History of Hindustan from the Most Early Ages to the End of the Marquis of Hastings Administration in 1823, Designed for the Use of*

Young Men Going-Out To India, London: Longman, Hurst, Rees, Orme, Brown and Green.

xvii. Waugh A. (1907), 'Providence', *The Poems of George Herbert with an Introduction by Arthur Waugh*, Oxford University Press, pp. 123.

7.   Fun with Trees in Art and Play

i.   Caine W.S. (1819), *Picturesque India: A Handbook for European Travellers*, London: George Routledge and Sons.

ii.   Ebifa-Othieno E., Mugisha A., Nyeko P., Kabasa D.J. (2017), 'Knowledge, Attitudes and Practices in Tamarind (*Tamarindus indica* L.): Use and Conservation in Eastern Uganda', *Journal of Ethnobiology and Ethnomedicine* 13 (5): pp. 13.

iii.   UNESCO, 'Ei-sok (Tamarind Seed Fetching)'.

8.   Tamarind: The Firangi Indica

i.   Adiga M. (2006), *The Making of Southern Karnataka: Society, Polity and Culture in the Early Medieval Period AD 400–1030*, Hyderabad: Orient Longman.

ii.   Anon. (1910), *The Gazetteer of Bombay City and Island (Vol. III)*, Bombay: Times Press.

iii.   Beverdige A.S. (1922), *The Babur-Nama in English (Memoirs of Babur)* (vol. II), translated from the original Turki text of Zahir'd-din Muhammad Babur Padshah Ghazi, London: Luzac & Co.

iv.   Bowe P. (2009), 'The Genius of an Artist: William R. Mustoe and the Planning of the City of New Delhi and Its Gardens', *Garden History* 37 (1): pp. 68–79.

v.   Cohen B. (2011), 'Modernising the Urban Environment: The Musi River Flood of 1908 in Hyderabad, India', *Environment and History* 17 (3): pp. 409–32.

vi.   Deloche J. (1993), *Transport and Communications in India Prior to Steam Locomotion* (vol. I): *Land Transport* (translated from the French by James Walker), Oxford University Press.

vii.   Edwards S.M. (1909), *The Gazetteer of Bombay City and Island* (vol I), Bombay: Cosmo Publications.

viii.   El-Siddig K., Gunasena H.P.M., Prasad B.A., et al. (2006), Tamarind (*Tamarindus indica*), International Centre for Underutilised Crops, University of Southampton, United Kingdom.

ix.   Forbes J. (1834), *Oriental Memoirs: A Narrative of Seventeen Years Residence in India* (vol. II), London: Richard Bentley.

x.   Hiwale S. (2015), *Sustainable Horticulture in Semi-Arid Dry Lands*, New Delhi: Springer India.

xi.   Karnataka State Archives (1887), 'Nallur Amarai Tope in Devanhalli Taluk', Land Revenue 1887/ 23 of 1887/1–27, Vidhan Soudha, Bengaluru.

xii.   National Research Council of the National Archives (2008), *Lost Crops of Africa* (vol. III), Washington DC: The National Academic Press.

xiii.   Oza G.M. (1978), 'Seed Shapes in *Tamarindus indica*', *Indian Forester* 104 (5): pp. 331–32.

xiv.   Roy B. (2004), 'Democracy Under the Tamarind Trees', *India International Centre Quarterly* 31(1): pp. 117–24.

xv.   Roy K. (2009) *Historical Dictionary of Ancient India*, Maryland: The Scarecrow Press.

xvi.   Shah N.C. (2014), '*Tamarindus indica*: Introduction in India and Culinary, Medicinal and Industrial Uses', *Asian Agri-History* 18(4): pp. 343–55.

xvii.   Subbarayalu (2014), *Dr H.F.C. Cleghorn: Founder of Forest Conservancy in India*, Chennai: Notion Press.

xviii. Times Press (1910), *The Gazetteer of Bombay City and Island* (vol. III), Bombay: Times Press.

9. Trees and the Environment

i. Chakre O.J. (2006), 'Choice of Eco-Friendly Trees in Urban Environment to Mitigate Airborne Particulate Pollution', *Journal of Human Ecology* 20(2): pp. 135–38.

ii. Dahiya S., Myllyvirta L., Sivalingam N. (2017), 'Apocalypse: Assessment of Air Pollution in Indian Cities', Greenpeace India.

iii. Dar S.R. (2000), 'Caravansarais along the Grand Trunk Road in Pakistan: A Central Asian Legacy', *The Silk Roads: Highways of Culture and Commerce* (ed. Elisseeff V), pp. 158–84, Paris: UNESCO.

iv. Endreny T., Santagata R., Perna A. et al (2017), 'Implementing and Managing Urban Forests: A Much-Needed Conservation Strategy to Increase Ecosystem Services and Urban Wellbeing', *Ecological Modelling* 360: pp. 328–35.

v. Frost R. (1946), 'The Sound of the Trees', *The Poems of Robert Frost*, New York: The Modern Library, pp. 175.

vi. Karnataka State Archives (1876), 'Letter from the Conservator of Forests Mysore and Coorg', no. 2375, dated 7 January 1876, Proceedings of the Chief Commissioner of Mysore, General Department, 21 January 1876, Vidhan Soudha, Bengaluru.

vii. McDonald R., Kroeger T., Boucher T., et al. (2016), 'Planting Healthy Air: A Global Analysis of the Role of Urban Trees in Addressing Particulate Matter Pollution and Extreme Heat', The Nature Conservancy.

viii. Mohammad W. (1941), 'Beautiful Trees: Their Planting and Care', *Indian Forester* 67(11): pp. 575–88.

ix.   Nuwer R. (2013), 'Trees Make Noises and Some of These Sounds are Cries for Help', Smithsonian.com, 16 April 2013.

x.   Prasad R., Pandey R.K. (1985), 'Methyl-Isocyanate (MIC) Hazard to the Vegetation of Bhopal', *Journal of Tropical Forestry* 1(1): pp. 40–50.

xi.   Shannigrahi A.S., Fukushima T., Sharma R.C. (2004), 'Anticipated Air Pollution Tolerance of Some Plant Species Considered for Green Belt Development in and Around an Industrial/Urban Area in India: An Overview', *International Journal of Environmental Studies* 61(2): pp. 125–37.

xii. Song X.P., Tan P.Y., Edwards P., Richards D. (2018), 'The Economic Benefits and Costs of Trees in Urban Forest Stewardship: A Systematic Review', *Urban Forestry and Urban Greening* 29: pp. 162–70.

xiii. Vailshery L.S., Jaganmohan M., Nagendra H. (2013), 'Effect of Street Trees on Microclimate and Air Pollution in a Tropical City', *Urban Forestry and Urban Greening* 12: pp. 408–15.

10. The Great Eucalyptus Debate

i.   Beattie J. (2011), *Empire and Environmental Anxiety: Health, Art, Science and Conservation in South Asia and Australasia 1800–1920*, Hampshire: Palgrave Macmillan.

ii.   Bhojvaid P.P., Kaushik S., Singh Y.P., Kumar D., Thapliyal M., Barthwal S. (eds) (2014), *Eucalyptus in India*, ENVIS Centre on Forestry.

iii. Coppen J.J.W. (ed) (2002), *Eucalyptus: The Genus Eucalyptus*, London and New York: Taylor & Francis.

iv.   Devi M. (1983), 'Why Eucalyptus?', *Economic and Political Weekly* 18(32): pp. 1379–381.

v.   Doughty R.W. (2000), *The Eucalyptus: A Natural and Commercial History of the Gum Tree*, Baltimore and London: The John Hopkins University Press.

vi.   Freer-Smith P.H., El-khatib A., Taylor G. (2004), 'Capture of Particulate Pollution by Trees: A Comparison of Species Typical of Semi-Arid Areas (*Ficus nitida* and *Eucalyptus globulus*) with European and North American Species', *Water, Air and Soil Pollution* 155: pp. 173–87.

vii. Gamble J.S. (1882) (ed), 'Malaria and the Value of Eucalyptus', *Indian Forester* 7: pp. 335–40.

viii. Kumar N. (2014), 'A Study of Resource Selection by Black Kites, *Milvus migrans*, in the Urban Landscape of the National Capital Region, India'. Final project report submitted to Wildlife Institute of India, Dehradun.

ix.   Ministry of Urban Development (2014), Urban Greening Guidelines 2014, Town and Country Planning Organisation, Ministry of Urban Development, Government of India.

x.   Palanna M. (1993), 'Eucalyptus in India', reports submitted to the regional expert consultation on eucalyptus (vol. II), FAO regional office for Asia and the Pacific, Bangkok.

xi.   Pandit R. (2018), 'Why Eucalyptus?', *Down to Earth*, 19 September 2018

xii. Randhawa M.S. (1946), 'A Tree Plantation Plan for Northern India', *Indian Forester* 72(2): 107–10.

xiii. Shiva V., Bandyopadhyay J. (1987), 'Ecological Audit of Eucalyptus Cultivation', Research Foundation for Science and Ecology, Dehradun.

xiv. Srinivasan V., Thompson S., Madhyastha K., et al. (2015), 'Why Is the Arkavathy River Drying? A Multiple-Hypothesis Approach in a Data Scarce Region', *Hydrology and Earth System Sciences* 19: pp. 1905–917.

xv.   Sunder S.S. (1985), 'Urban Tree Planting: Foresters Efforts in Bangalore', *Indian Forster* 112(4): pp. 296–304.

xvi. Tewari T.N. (1992), *Monograph on Eucalyptus*, Dehradun: Surya Publications.

11. Sacred and Venerable

i. Bell K.L., Rangan H., Kull C.A., Murphy D.J. (2015), 'The History of Introduction of the African Baobab (*Adansonia digitata*, Malvaceae, Bombacoideae) in the Indian Subcontinent', *The Royal Society Open Science* 2: 150370 pp.15.

ii. Institution of Foresters (2009), 'Sacred Groves in Trissur District', Trivandrum, Kerala.

iii. Musselman L.J. (2003), 'Trees in the Koran and the Bible', *Unasylva* 213(54): pp. 8.

iv. Rau M.A. (1967), 'The Sacred Mulberry Tree of Joshimath U.P.', *Indian Forester* 93(8): pp. 533–34.

v. Sagwal S.S. (1996), 'Management of Chinar (*Platanus orientalis* L.)', *Ecofriendly Trees for Urban Beautification* (eds. Khosla P.K., Uppal D.K., Sharma R.K., et al.), Solan: Indian Institute of Tree Scientists and Gurgaon: National Horticultural Board.

vi. Sastry V.P.S. (2000), 'Baobab: The Wishing Tree', *Asian Agri-History* 4(4): pp. 315–18.

vii. Sorenson J.L. (2005), 'Ancient Voyages Across the Ocean to America: From "Impossible" to "Certain"', *Journal of Book of Mormon Studies* 14(1): pp. 6–17.

viii. Thiruvady V., *Heritage Trees in and around Bangalore*, Bangalore: Bangalore Environment Trust.

ix. Upadhyaya K.D. (1964), 'Indian Botanical Folklore', *Asian Folklore Studies* 23(2): pp. 15–34.

x. Waterfield W. (1913), *Indian Ballads*. Allahabad: Panini Office.

12. Amaltas: Golden Chandeliers with Buzzing Bees

i. Buchanan F. (1807), *A Journey from Madras, through the Countries of Mysore, Canara and Malabar*, London: printed for T. Cadell and W. Davies (Booksellers to the Asiatic Society) in the Strand; and Black Parry and Kingsbury (Booksellers to the East India Company) in Leadenhall Street.

ii. Buchmann S.L. (1983), 'Buzz Pollination in Angiosperms', *Handbook of Experimental Pollination Biology* (eds. Jones C.E., Little R.J.), New York: Van Nostrand Reinhold Company, pp. 73–113.

iii. De Luca P.A., Vallejo-Marin M. (2013), 'What's the "Buzz" About? The Ecology and Evolutionary Significance of Buzz Pollination', *Current Opinion in Plant Biology* 16(4): pp. 429–35.

iv. Dikshitar V.R.R. (translator) (1939), *The Śilappadikāram*, Oxford University Press.

v. Edwards S.M. (1909), *The Gazetteer of Bombay City and Island* (vol. I), Bombay: Cosmo Publications.

vi. Freitas B.M., Pereira J.O.P. (2004), 'Solitary Bees: Conservation, Rearing and Management for Pollination', a contribution to the International Workshop on Solitary Bees and Their Role in Pollination, held in Beberibe, Ceará, Brazil, April 2004.

vii. Karnataka State Archives (1873), A letter from Deputy Commissioner of Mysore District to the Off. Commissioner of Ashtagram Division no. 253, dated 23 June 1873, in the Proceedings of the Chief Commissioner of Mysore, Department of Agriculture, Revenue and Commerce 13 August 1873.

viii. Keyser P., Irby-Massie G. (2008), *The Encyclopaedia of Ancient Natural Scientists: The Greek Tradition and Its Many Heirs*, Oxon: Routledge.

ix. Murali K.S. (1993), 'Differential Reproductive Success in *Cassia fistula* in Different Habitats: A Case of Pollinator Limitation?' *Current Science* 65(3): pp. 270–72.

x.   Naidu S. (1928), 'Golden Cassia', *The Sceptred Flute: Songs of India*, New York: Dodd, Mead & Company, pp. 96.

xi. North M. (1894), *Recollections of a Happy Life: Being the Autobiography of Marianne North,* edited by her sister, Mrs John Addington Symonds (vol. II), New York: Macmillan & Co.

xii. Russell R.V. (1916), *The Tribes and Castes of the Central Provinces of India* (vol. III), London: Macmillan & Co.

xiii. Singh A. (2010), 'Wildlife in Mughal India from Text and Paintings', PhD. thesis, Aligarh Muslim University, Aligarh.

xiv. Troup R.S. (1921), *The Silviculture of Indian Trees: Leguminosae (Caesalpinieae) to Verbenaceae* (vol. II), Oxford University Press.

13. Native and Exotic: Identity Crises of Trees

i.   Ahuja S.C., Ahuja S., Ahuja U. (2014), 'Coconut: History, Uses and Folklore', *Asian Agri-History* 18 (3): 21–48..

ii. Brockway L.H. (1979), 'Science and Colonial Expansion: The Role of the British Royal Botanic Gardens', *American Ethnologist* 6(3): pp. 449–65.

iii. Davis M. (2011), 'Don't Judge Species on Their Origin', *Nature* 474: pp. 153–54.

iv. Geesing D., Al-Khawlani M., Abba M.L. (2004), 'Management of Introduced Prosopis species: Can Economic Exploitation Control Invasive Species', *Unasylva* 55: pp. 36–44.

v.   Lucy V. (2010), 'An Historical Geography of the Nilgiri Cinchona Plantations (1860–1900)', PhD. thesis, University of Nottingham.

vi. Osborne M.A. (2000), 'Acclimatizing the World: A History of the Paradigmatic Colonial Science', *Osiris* 15: pp. 135–51.

vii.   Pasiecznik N.M., Felker P., Harris P.J.C., et al. (2001), *Prosopis juliflora – Prosopis pallida Complex: A Monograph*, HDRA Coventry, United Kingdom.

viii. Philip K. (1995), 'Imperial Science Rescues a Tree: Global Botanic Networks, Local Knowledge and the Transcontinental Transportation of Cinchona', *Environment and History* 1(2): pp. 173–200.

ix.   Rangan H., Kull C.A., Alexander L. (2010), 'Forest Plantations, Water Availability, and Regional Climate Change: Controversies Surrounding *Acacia mearnsii* Plantations in the Upper Palni Hills, Southern India', *Regional Environmental Change* 10 (2): pp. 103–17.

14.   The Scarlet Silk Cotton

i.   Baker H.G., Harris, B.J. (1959), 'Bat Pollination of the Silk-Cotton Tree, *Ceiba pentandra* (L.) Gaertn. (sensu lato), in Ghana', *Journal of the West African Science Association* 4: pp. 1–9.

ii.   Bhattacharya A., Mandal S. (2000), 'Pollination Biology in *Bombax ceiba* Linn', *Current Science* 79(12): pp. 1706–712.

iii.   Farooq M., Saxena R.P., Beg M.U. (1988), 'Sulphur Dioxide Resistance of Indian Trees', *Water, Air and Soil Pollution* 40: pp. 307–16.

iv.   Howe M.A. (1906), 'Some Photographs of the Silk Cotton Tree (*Ceiba pentandra*) with Remarks on the Early Records of its Occurrence in America', *Torreya* 6(11): pp. 217–31.

v.   Jain V., Verma S.K., Katewa S.S. (2009), 'Myths, Traditions and Fate of Multipurpose *Bombax ceiba* L.: An Appraisal', *Indian Journal of Traditional Knowledge* 8(4): pp. 638–44.

vi.   Kusugal A. (2013), 'Genetic Studies on Improving Productivity, Fibre Quality Traits and Combining Ability in Barbadense Cotton (*Gossypium barbadense* L.)', Masters thesis submitted to the University of Agricultural Sciences, Dharwad.

vii.   Macauliffe M.A. (1909), *The Sikh Religion: Its Gurus, Sacred Writings and Authors* (vol. 1), Oxford: Clarendon Press.

viii.   Singh J. (2005), 'Ethics of the Sikhs', *Understanding Sikhism: The Research Journal* 7 (1): pp. 35–38.

ix.   The Indian Textile Journal (1916), 'Semul or Silk Cotton', *Indian Forester* 42 (2): pp. 102.

15.   The Fellowship of the Grove

i.   'Eha' Aitken E.H. (1904), *The Tribes on My Frontier: Indian Naturalists Foreign Policy*, London: W. Thacker & Co.

ii.   African Development Fund (2016), Accra Urban Transport Project, Project Appraisal Report.

iii.   Ameyaw A.A., Raheem K. (2008), 'Indigenous Methods for Effective Sustainable Utilisation of Environmental Resources in Developing Countries', *Teaching and Education for Teaching in Developing Countries*, (eds. Garuba A., Irwin L). University of Education, Winneba, Ghana, pp. 125–32.

iv.   Baviskar A. (2018), 'Urban Jungles: Wilderness, Parks and Their Publics in Delhi', *Economic and Political Weekly* 53(2): pp. 46–54.

v.   Bond R. (1975), *The World of Trees*, New Delhi: National Book Trust.

vi.   Drake-Brockman D.L. (1909), *Jhansi: A Gazetteer being* (vol. xxiv) *of the District Gazetteers of the United Provinces of Agra and Oudh*, Allahabad: Government Press.

vii.   Edwards S.M. (1909), *The Gazetteer of Bombay City and Island* (vol. I), Bombay: Cosmo Publications.

viii.   Forbes J. (1834), *Oriental Memoirs: A Narrative of Seventeen Years Residence in India* (vol. II), London: Richard Bentley.

ix.   Houlton J. (1949), *Bihar: The Heart of India,* Bombay, Calcutta, Madras: Orient Longmans Ltd.

x.   Muter (1864), *Travels and Adventures in India, China and New Zealand* (vol. I), London: Hurst and Blackett Publishers.

xi.   Nene Y.L. (2001), 'Mango through Millennia', *Asian Agri-History* 5(1): pp. 39–67.

xii.   Nevill H.R. (1904), *Lucknow: A Gazetteer being* (vol. xxxvii) *of the District Gazetteers of the United Provinces of Agra and Oudh*, Allahabad: Government Press.

xiii.   Nevill H.R. (1905) *Agra: A Gazetteer being* (vol. iii) *of the District Gazetteers of the United Provinces of Agra and Oudh*, Allahabad: Government Press.

xiv.   Nevill H.R. (1909) *Cawnpore: A Gazetteer being* (vol. xix) *of the District Gazetteers of the United Provinces of Agra and Oudh*, Allahabad: Government Press

xv.   Pharaoh & Co. (1855), *A Gazetteer of Southern India with the Tenasserium Provinces and Singapore Compiled from Original and Authentic Sources Accompanied by an Atlas Including of All the Principal Towns and Cantonment,* Madras.

xvi.   Rice B.L. (1897), *Mysore: A Gazetteer Compiled for Government* (vol. I and II), Westminster: Archibald Constable and Company.

xvii.   Singh C., Wattas R., Dhillon H.S. (1998), *Trees of Chandigarh,* New Delhi: B.R. Publishing Corporation.

xviii.   Sleeman W.H. (1844), *Rambles and Recollections of an Indian Official* (vol. I), London: J. Hatchard & Son.

xix.   Thapar R. (2002), *The Penguin History of Early India: From the Origins to AD 1300,* New Delhi: Penguin India.

16. Neem: The Bitter Tree of Wellness

i. Achaya K.T. (1992), 'Indian Oilpress (Ghani)', *Indian Journal of History of Science* 27(1): pp. 5–13.

ii. Ahmed M. (2014), *Ancient Pakistan-An Archaeological History: Vol IV Harappan Civilization-Theoretical and the Abstract*, Foursome Group.

iii. Ahmed S., Bamofleh S., Munshi M. (1989), 'Cultivation of Neem (*Azadirachta indica*, Meliaceae) in Saudi Arabia', *Economic Botany* 43(1): pp. 35–38.

iv. Caspers E.C.L.D. (1992), 'Rituals and Belief Systems in the Indus Valley Civilisation', *Ritual, State and History in South Asia: Essays in Honour of J.C. Heesterman* (eds. Van Den Hoek A. W., Kolff D. H. A., Oort M. S.), Lieden, New York and Koln: E.J. Brill, pp. 102–27.

v. Desmond K. (2017), *Planet Savers: 301 Extraordinary Environmentalists*, London and New York: Routledge Taylor and Francis Group.

vi. Elwood A.K. (1830), *Narrative of a Journey Overland from England by the Continent of Europe, Egypt and the Red Sea to India, Including a Residence and Voyage Home in the Years 1825, 26, 27 and 28* (vol. 1), London: Henry Colburn and Richard Bentley.

vii. Granziera P. (2010), 'The Indo-Mediterranean Caduceus and the Worship of the Tree, the Serpent, and the Mother Goddess in the South of India', *Comparative Studies of South Asia, Africa and the Middle East* 3(3): pp. 610–20.

viii. Hellerer U., Jayaraman K.S. (2000), 'Greens Persuade Europe to Revoke Patent on Neem', *Nature* 405: pp. 266-67.

ix. Laurie M.V. (1939), 'Germination of Nim Seeds (*Azadirachta indica*)', *Indian Forester* 65(2): pp. 104–06.

x.   Marden E. (1999), 'The Neem Tree Patent: International Conflict Over the Commodification of Life', *Boston College International and Comparative Law Review* 22(2): pp. 279–95.

xi.   Nagendra Prasad M.N., Bhat S.S., Nanjundappa H., et al (2010), 'Study of Die-Back Disease Incidence of Neem in Karnataka India and PCR-based Identification of the Isolates', *Archives of Phytopathology and Plant Protection* 4(5): pp. 446–53.

xii.   Omkar G.M. (2012), 'Neem the Wonder Tree under Attack: A New Major Pest', *Current Science* 102(7): pp. 969–70.

xiii.   Patil J. (1996), *Agricultural and Rural Reconstruction: A Sustainable Approach*, New Delhi: Concept Publishing Company.

xiv.   Puri H.S. (1999), *Neem: The Divine Tree*, Hardwood Academic Publishers.

xv.   Rawat G.S. (1995), 'Neem (*Azadirachta indica*): Nature's Drugstore', *Indian Forester* 121(11): pp. 977–80.

xvi.   Saraswat K.S. (1992), 'Archaeobotanical Remains in Ancient Cultural and Socio-Economical Dynamics of the Indian Subcontinent', *Palaeobotanist* 40: pp. 514-45.

17.   An Inordinate Fondness for Trees

i.   Daane K.M., Sime K.R., Dahlsten D.L., et al. (2005), 'The Biology of *Psyllaephagus bliteus* Riek (Hymenoptera: Encyrtidae), a Parasitoid of the Red Gum Lerp Psyllid (Hemiptera: Psylloidea)', *Biological Control* 32(2): pp. 228–35.

ii.   Garnier E., Navas M., Grigulis K. (2016), *Plant Functional Diversity: Organism Traits, Community Structure, and Ecosystem Properties*, Oxford: Oxford University Press.

iii.   Hugo N.R. (2011), *Seeing Trees: Discover the Extraordinary Secrets of Everyday Trees*, Oregon: Timber Press.

iv.   Junker R.R., Parachnowitsch A.L. (2015), 'Working towards a Holistic View on Flower Traits: How Floral Scents Mediate Plant–Animal Interactions in Concert with Other Floral Characters', *Journal of the Indian Institute of Science* 95(1): pp. 43–68.

v.   Junker R.R., Parachnowitsch A.L. (2015), 'Working towards a Holistic View on Flower Traits', *Journal of the Indian Institute of Science* 95(1): pp. 43–67.

vi.   Paine T.D., Dreistadt S.H. Garrison R.W., Gill R.J. (2006), 'Eucalyptus Red Gum Lerp Psyllid', Pest Notes Publication 746, University of California Agriculture and Natural Resources.

vii.   'TRY: Plant Trait Database Hosted by Future Earth and the Max Planck Institute for Biogeochemistry', https://www.try-db.org/TryWeb/Home.php.

18.   Peepul: The People's Tree

i.   Bond R. (1975), *The World of Trees*, New Delhi: National Book Trust.

ii.   Nene Y.L. (2001), 'Trees in Ancient Literature: II, The Pipal Tree', *Asian Agri-History* 5(2): pp. 141–48.

iii.   Watts G. (1890), *A Dictionary of the Economic Products of India* (vol. III), New Delhi: Cosmo Publications.

19.   Tree-Deficit Disorder

i.   Adjuntament de Barcelona (2017), 'Trees for Life: Masterplan for Barcelona's Trees 2017–2037'.

ii.   Bratman G.N., Hamilton J.P., Daily G.C. (2012), 'The Impacts of Nature Experience on Human Cognitive Function and Mental Health', *Annals of the New York Academy of Sciences* 1249: pp. 118–36.

iii.   Chen W.Y. (forthcoming), 'Recreational Values of Urban Nature', *Routledge Handbook of Urban Ecology* (second edition).

iv.   Dwyer F.J., McPherson E.G., Schroeder H.W., Rowntree R.A. (1992), 'Assessing the Benefits and Costs of the Urban Forest', *Journal of Arboriculture* 18(5): pp. 227–34.

v.   Forest Research (2010), 'Benefits of Green Infrastructure', report by Forest Research, Farnham.

vi.   Hartig T., Mitchell R., de Vries S., Frumkin H. (2014), 'Nature and Health', *Annual Review of Public Health* 35: pp. 207–28.

vii.   Jiang B., Li D., Larsen L., et al. (2014), 'A Dose–Response Curve Describing the Relationship between Urban Tree Cover Density and Self-Reported Stress Recovery', *Environment and Behavior* 48(4): pp. 607–29.

viii.   LeBlanc A.G., Katzmarzyk P.T., Barreira T.V., et al. (2015), 'Correlates of Total Sedentary Time and Screen Time in 9 - 11-year-old Children around the World: The International Study of Childhood Obesity, Lifestyle and the Environment', *PLoS ONE* 10(6): e012962.

ix.   Louv R. (2008), *Last Child in the Woods: Saving Our Children from Nature-Deficit Disorder,* North Carolina: Algonquin Books of Chapel Hill.

x.   Malhotra K.C., Kumar V. (1987), 'A Socio-Ecological Study of the Avenue Trees of Calcutta', *Ecology of Urban India Vol. II* (ed. Singh P), New Delhi: Ashish Publishing House, pp. 144–68.

xi.   Neralu: The Bengaluru Tree Festival, http://neralu.in/.

xii.   Richardson M., McEwan K., Garip G. (2018), '30 Days Wild: Who Benefits Most?', *Journal of Public Mental Health* 17(3): pp. 95–104.

xiii.   Shanahan D.F., Bush B., Gaston K.J. et al. (2016), 'Health Benefits from Nature Experiences Depends on Dose', *Scientific Reports* 6, article no. 28551.

xiv.   Shri Krishan (2011), 'Water Harvesting Traditions and the Social Milieu in India: A Second Look', *Economic and Political Weekly* 46 (26 and 27): pp. 87–94.

xv.   Tilt J.H., Cerveny L.K. (forthcoming), 'Urban Nature and Human Physical Health', *Routledge Handbook of Urban Ecology* (second edition).

xvi.   Wilson E.O. (1984), *Biophilia*, Cambridge: Harvard University Press.

20.   Drum Roll for the Drumstick

i.   Anwar F., Latif S., Ashraf M., Gilani A.H. (2007), '*Moringa oleifera*: A Food Plant with Multiple Medicinal Uses', *Phototherapy Research* 21: pp. 17–25.

ii.   Chukwuebuka E. (2015), '*Moringa oleifera*: "The mothers' best friend"', *International Journal of Nutrition and Food Sciences* 4(6): pp. 624–30.

iii.   Edwards S.M. (1909), *The Gazetteer of Bombay City and Island* (vol. I), Bombay: Cosmos Publications.

iv.   Gopalakrishnan L., Doriya K., Kumar D.S. (2016), '*Moringa oleifera*: A Review on Nutritive Importance and Its Medicinal Application', *Food Science and Human Wellness* 5: pp. 49–56.

v.   Gopalan C., Rama Sastri B.V., Balabsubramanian S.V. revised and updated by Narasinga Rao B.S., Deosthale Y.G., Pant K.C. (1989), *Nutritive Value of Indian Foods*, Hyderabad: National Institute of Nutrition. pp.47–58

vi.   Ntila S., Ndhlala A.R., Kolanisi U., et al. (2018), 'Acceptability of a Moringa-Added Complementary Soft Porridge to Caregivers in Hammanskraal, Gauteng Province, and Lebowakgomo, Limpopo Province, South Africa', *South African Journal of Clinical Nutrition* 1(1): pp. 1–7.

vii.   Parrotta J.A. (1993), '*Moringa oleifera*: Moringaceae Horse Radish Tree', report number: res. note SO-ITF-SM-61, affiliation: New Orleans, LA: US Department of Agriculture, Forest Service, Southern Forest Experiment Station.

viii.   Rockwood J.L., Anderson B.G., Casamatta D.A. (2013), 'Potential Uses of *Moringa oleifera* and an Examination of Antibiotic Efficacy', *International Journal of Phototherapy Research* 3: pp. 61–71.

ix.   Wyvern (1885), *Culinary Jottings: A Treatise in Thirty Chapters on Reformed Cookery for Anglo-Indian Rites Based upon Modern English and Continental Principles with Thirty Menus for Little Dinners Worked Out in Detail and an Essay on Our Kitchens in India*, Madras: Higginbothams.

x.   Zaku S.G., Emmanuel S., Tukur A.A., Kabir A. (2015), '*Moringa oleifera*: An Underutilised Tree in Nigeria with Amazing Versatility: A Review', *African Journal of Food Science* 9(9): pp. 456–61.

21.   Trees of Recipes and Remedies

i.   Edwards S.M. (1909), *The Gazetteer of Bombay City and Island* (vol. I).

ii.   Mollee E., McDonald M., Pouliot M. (2017), 'Into the Urban Wild: Collection of Wild Urban Plants for Food and Medicine in Kampala, Uganda', *Land Use Policy* 63: pp. 67–77.

iii.   Imran M., Arshad M.S., Butt M.S. et al (2017), 'Mangiferin: A Natural Miracle Bioactive Compound against Lifestyle-Related Disorders', *Lipids in Health and Disease* 16:84 pp. 17.

iv.   Khan A.S. (2017), *Medically Important Trees*, Springer International Publishing.

v.   Murugesan A. (1999), 'Plants in Tamil Proverbial Lore', *Pulamai* 25(2): pp. 4.

vi.   PETA (2017), 'Why Jackfruit Is the Hottest Food Trend of 2017'.

vii. Rao P.S. (1952), 'Non-cereal Foods: Tamarind Seed Kernels As Food and Fodder', *Indian Forester* 78(1): pp. 36–38.

viii. Sing B. (1951), 'A Mango Charm', *Indian Forester* 77(7): pp. 476.

22.   **What Lies Ahead?**

i.   eBird, https://ebird.org/home, hosted by Cornell Lab of Ornithology.

ii.   SeasonWatch, http://www.seasonwatch.in/, hosted in collaboration with National Centre for Biological Sciences (Tata Institute of Fundamental Research), Wipro, Nature Conservation Foundation, Matrubhoomi SEED, Green Schools Program and efloraofIndia.

iii. Inside Wood, http://insidewood.lib.ncsu.edu/, hosted by North Carolina State University.

iv.   Urban Slender Loris Project, http://www. urbanslenderlorisproject.org/, principal scientist Kaberi Kar Gupta.

BIBLIOGRAPHY

i.   Asouti E., Fuller D.Q. (2010), *Trees and Woodlands of South India: Archaeological Perspectives,* New Delhi: Munshiram Manoharlal Publishers Pvt. Ltd.

ii.   Benthall A.P. (1946), *Trees of Calcutta and Its Neighbourhood,* Calcutta: Thacker Spink & Co.

iii.   Blatter E., Millard W.S. (1954), *Some Beautiful Indian Trees,* Bombay: Bombay Natural History Society.

iv.   Bole P.V., Vaghani Y. (1986), *Field Guide to the Common Trees of India,* World Wide Fund for Nature India and Oxford University Press.

v.   Butterworth A. (1911), *Some Madras Trees,* Madras: Methodist Publishing House.

vi.   Colthurst I. (1924), *Familiar Flowering Trees in India,* Calcutta and Simla: Thacker, Spink & Co.

vii.   Cowen D.V. (1957), *Flowering Trees and Shrubs in India,* Bombay: Thaker & Co. Ltd.

viii.   Karthikeyan S. (2014), *Discover Avenue Trees: A Pocket Guide,* Bangalore: Ecoedu Consultants Pvt Ltd.

ix.   Kavitha A., Deepthi N., Ganesan R., Jospeh S.C.G. (2012), *Common Dryland Trees of Karnataka: Bilingual Field Guide,* Bangalore: Ashoka Trust for Research in Ecology and the Environment.

x.   Krishen P. (2006), *Trees of Delhi: A Field Guide,* Delhi: Dorling Kindersley (India) Pvt. Limited.

xi. Krishna N., Amirthalingam M. (2014), *Sacred Plants of India*, Gurgaon: Penguin Books.

xii. Lattoo C., Karnik M.D., Chaphekar S. (2007), *Sen 'trees' of Mumbai*, Mumbai: Mugdha Karnik for Mumbai University.

xiii. McCann C. (1959), *100 Beautiful Trees of India*, Bombay: D.B. Taraporevala Sons & Co. Pvt. Ltd.

xiv. Mukherjee P. (1983), *Common Trees of India*, World Wildlife Fund India and Oxford University Press.

xv. Nagendra H. (2016), *Nature in the City: Bengaluru in the Past, Present and Future*, New Delhi: Oxford University Press.

xvi. Nalini S. (tr.) (1996), *Surapala's Vrikshayurveda (The Science of Plant Life by Surapala)*, bulletin no. 1, Asian Agri-History Foundation, Secunderabad, India.

xvii. Neginhal S.G. (2006), *Golden Trees, Greenspaces and Urban Forestry*, self-published.

xviii. Prasanna P.V., Chandramohan Reddy N., Venkat Raman M., Venu P. (2014), *Trees of Hyderabad: A Pictorial Guide*, Kolkata: Botanical Survey of India.

xix. Randhawa M.S. (1957), *Flowering Trees of India*, New Delhi: Indian Council of Agricultural Research.

xx. Rao K.N. (2008), *Trees and Tree Tales: Some Common Trees of Chennai*, Oxygen Books

xxi. Sachdeva P., Tongbram V. (2017), *A Naturalist's Guide to the Trees and Shrubs of India, Pakistan, Nepal, Bhutan, Bangladesh and Sri Lanka*, New Delhi: Prakash Books.

xxii. Sahni K.C. (2000), *The Book of Indian Trees*, Bombay: Bombay Natural History Society.

xxiii. Santapau H. (2015), *Common Trees*, New Delhi: National Book Trust.

xxiv. Shanahan M. (2016), *Gods Wasps and Stranglers: The Secret History and Redemptive Future of Fig Trees,* Vermont: Chelsea Green Publishing.

ACKNOWLEDGEMENTS

It has been a real pleasure to work with our colleagues at Penguin Random House India; their enthusiasm is infectious. In particular, we thank Manasi Subramaniam, who worked closely with us from start to finish; Alisha Dutt Islam, whose superb illustrations enrich the book's pages; Gunjan Ahlawat for the design inputs; and Aslesha Kadian, for her thoughtful and thorough copy-editing. We also thank Samanth Subramanian for introducing us to Penguin.

Sreeranjini, Anora Lobo, Vinay Sankar, Chinta Prameela and Manish Chandi provided us with numerous interesting bits of information. Hita Unnikrishnan and B. Manjunath accompanied us on a number of memorable field trips. The superb library staff at Azim Premji University helped us track down a number of difficult references. We thank the Centre for Urban Sustainability in India, at Azim Premji University, for funding and supporting the extensive research that went into this book. We are especially appreciative of the supportive and stimulating environment that Azim Premji University provides us, which was ideal for writing a book of this nature.

Given a book of this scope, we have received a great deal of help along the way and have our own personal acknowledgements to add.

Harini

I am indebted to my family for sharing with me their love for trees. My mother-in-law, Annapurna, was a formidable gardener. Her connect with nature was imbibed from childhood, growing in a large family surrounded by trees. My family home in Salem also had a large garden, lovingly tended to by my grandmother, Thungabai. Her children inherited her green thumbs. My mother and aunts coax incredible quantities of flowers and fruits from their gardens! My mother passed on her love for trees to me, and it is a pleasure to do the same with my daughter, Dhwani. The descriptions of mangoes in this book are for my sister Anjana, in tribute to Amma's mango tree, which showers us with hundreds of mangoes when in the mood.

Lakshmi feeds our zest for trees and flowers, foraging and bringing in new flowers to admire and record. Appa and Baba, constant champions of all my projects, would have been very pleased to see yet another book taking shape. And, of course, this book could never have been written without the support of Venkatachalam Suri, my steadfast companion on tree walks and journeys of discovery for over twenty-five years, and Dhwani, my biggest cheerleader.

Seema

Thank you Hita for cheerfully agreeing to take the author photograph for this book. Thank you to friends and family for their support and affection over the years. My parents, Narayanan and Savithry, who unfailingly took my brother and me to our ancestral home in Kerala. Those summer holidays, spent amidst nature, have left an indelible mark. Madhavi and Ram — you have not only been a part of some enjoyable trips, but have also been a huge source of support to me. Madhuri Ramesh — what would I have done without your insightful comments on all things relevant and irrelevant. Prema Naraynen — thank you for being on speed dial for queries related to writing, publishing and, most importantly, pet care. Mykah and Fuzzy — you came towards the later months of writing this book, but you took over with admirable efficiency — marking all mails as important by walking over the keyboard — and ensuring that I did more than just focus on the book.

Finally, my prop roots — Venku and Ravi. Venku — you have been the most supportive partner. Thank you so much for the affection and steadying hand over all these years. Ravi — my brother and friend in whose company the seeds of my love for nature was sown. When I look back, you have always been there sharing in my happiest moments and looking out for me, always, in my harder days.